I Am Real

By Glennys Hyland

VIDE

Dedication

This book is dedicated to God—my heavenly Father—to my Lord and Savior, Jesus Christ, and to the Holy Spirit, because without them, I would not be able to experience what I have experienced here on earth. A life with a purpose, full of an inexplicable and eternal joy!

To my husband Shawn, a living representation of the Scriptures. A man of integrity, humility, and full of love and compassion. A man who puts God and others before himself. Everything he does, he does it for the glory of God and not man.

To my five children, you have all been my training field. I put in practice what I learned in the Scriptures. Sometimes I failed the test, but many times I passed. Thank you for your grace, love, forgiveness, and your understanding that even though I did not know what I was doing, or how to do it. I trusted my Teacher, my Master, and my Helper and that works and continues working.

To the woman (Miriam) who knocked at my door and introduced me to her "perfect love—Jesus Christ." You told me that I was a seed and that you'll see the fruits. Here they are. Wherever you are, know that I am forever thankful for you!

My apologies to God for telling Him that He was not real but merely a man-made statue. You have proved to me, and I am convinced with my own life that You, the I AM, who sent me here to this earth, are REAL!

Introduction

I'm bringing you to this country so you can tell everyone that you get in contact with, that I AM REAL. These are the words I heard many years ago while sitting in a quiet and dark airplane, coming to America for the first time. While everyone slept, I was crying tears of joy, feeling as if I just got liberated, as if the shackles were falling off my hands. I remembered in the middle of my brokenness silently telling God to never bring me back, to bury my past and change my heart. To change my life. I was ready and excited to start all over and to heal the bruises and erase the scars. What I didn't know was that I just started a journey that would confirm what He just asked me to do. "Tell everyone that you get in contact with that I am real." Just as God has been real in my life, I want to be real in yours through this book by sharing all of my experiences with Him, the I AM" (Exodus 3:14).

As a little girl I had a lot of questions to ask God. When I visited the church, it was hard for me to concentrate because I was so sure that people were worshiping and trusting a God that was merely dead statues and empty religion. For some reason, my life experience revealed to me that the God I was to worship, the one my family was presenting to me, couldn't hear me, talk to me, or defend me. I wrote letters to Jesus, telling Him what was in my heart. My letters included statements such as, "I don't believe in you" and "You're not real". Then I would sneak to the back of the line of people bringing their offerings to the collection box under the statue of Jesus inside my small-town Catholic church. When it was my turn at the collection box, instead of depositing money, I deposited my letters. With an attitude of disappointment, I touched the feet of the statue, saying, "Read it." Then I would run away. (Exodus 22:23)

I needed an explanation. How was it possible for a God to exist if He allowed a little girl to be separated from her mother after seeing the destruction of her entire family? How could she believe that there was a God who claimed to be real while she was trying to survive in a world full of ungodly people? Instead of comfort and protection, they abused or tried to "abuse" her. She had no time to be a "little girl." Instead of playing with dolls, she needed to grow up quickly to deal with things that only adults should deal with. (Matthew 7:26–27)

Obviously, that statue could not respond, nor defend me, nor make me feel safe, but that was the God I knew. I became a young lady who ran to whoever's arms were open for me. After all, I was desperate for attention. I was desperate for love and for someone who could protect me from all the sources that increased my fears. My mind was saturated with memories that confused me and caused me to repeatedly make wrong decisions. Rebellion and anger were tainted medicine to soothe the agony, pain, confusion, and rejection that overflowed from my heart. (Leviticus 26:1; Exodus 3:7)

As a young woman, I was looking for answers and comfort. I visited someone who I thought could help me by telling my future. I visited a psychic who told me three major things that would happen in my life. The first two things were great things, but the third one was not. But I didn't care, as long I could hold on to the first two things to happen, I was OK. I kindly accepted her words and she gave me hope for my future. What I didn't know is that this was a trap of Satan to destroy my life, but God! (Leviticus 19:31; Deuteronomy 18:10–12).

By the age of twenty-two, I was a single mother of a beautiful little girl, but I was living with a married man that was not her father. He was in that city finishing his career at the university. After graduation, his plan was to go back to his family. Everything seemed so beautiful until the day I was kicked out of his house and once again I felt hopeless. This time, I found myself in the streets of one of the most dangerous cities in Honduras. I thought this was going to be my life until a young lady passing by recognized me and refused to leave me there. She brought me to her home. In a week, she realized that something wasn't right, and she brought me something that confirmed her assumption–a pregnancy test. The test gave me a positive result. At this point, I needed immediate help, so once again I wrote a letter, this one was to my oldest brother asking him for help and for forgiveness. Moved by my words and without hesitation, my brother came to get me and my daughter and brought us to his home (Psalm 68:5–6; Deuteronomy 31:6).

It was in my brother's house that I experienced God's presence for the first time. (If I ever came to you or to your door, asking to pray for you, this next paragraph will explain everything). One normal day, a lady did the inexplicable. While I was living life in my own way and strength and still empty inside, she knocked at my door, saying that God sent her to pray for me, and that's exactly what she did. She prayed for me and blessed me many times. She told me that I was a seed planted on her ground and that she would see the fruits. I was so ignorant of all of these things. I couldn't understand anything. I only knew that she came into my life at the right time and that she had something that no one else had — love at no cost. She was not ashamed of the gospel (Romans 1:16).

She invited me to her church youth group, and after watching a movie about the Rapture, the pastor asked if there was anyone who wanted to receive Jesus as their Lord and Savior. I honestly didn't know what this meant, and I was scared. I thought, what if this is a cult? What if they just want to abuse me? I wanted to raise my hand, but something was pulling it down and didn't let me pick it up. However, that same lady came to me and gently grabbed my hand and picked it up for me and I repeated the sinner's prayer. Everybody celebrated but me. Deep in my heart I was confused. I didn't know what was happening. What did I just do? Or why did I do it? Why couldn't I lift my hand myself? What was pulling my hand down? And why did she come and pick it up very easily? That movie convicted me of my sins, and I was afraid of going to that place called hell, so I was glad I lifted my hand up and confessed that Jesus is my Lord and Savior (Romans 10:9–10).

A week later I had a dream. Everything was happening so quickly; I was afraid I was losing my mind. In my dream, I felt like I was leaving reality. I was outside looking in on everything that was happening. I was pregnant (which I was for real) and I was asleep in my room at my brother's house. Suddenly, I heard the door open very slowly. I woke up and looked. It was Jesus coming into the room. Immediately I started to scream at him all of my life disappointments, just as I did in the letters. Jesus was walking very slowly and gently. I wanted Him to run to me, so I started to yield to Him. I was saying, "Come over here, Jesus. You are the one I want to hear." But He didn't react to my yielding. He continued walking slowly and gently. That really bothered me, so I screamed louder and started to ask, "Why? Why did these things happen to me? Why, Jesus, why?" (Psalm 61:2; 120:1; 130:1).

He continued walking slowly and gently. Not my cry, nor my yelling, nor my pain made Him run to me. Finally, He got to my bed and I moved to one side, making room for Him to sit next to me. When He sat close to me, I couldn't talk. There were no words. He grabbed my head and put it on His chest and with His hand rubbed my head. I felt a great and inexplicable peace (Philippians 4:7).

The next morning, something was different. The sunshine was shining inside that room like never before, and on my bed, there was a print as if someone sat there the whole night. Honestly, all of these experiences made me feel very fearful. I thought I was going crazy. I couldn't even tell anybody what had happened to me because I thought that they would lock me in a psychiatric hospital. So, I kept this dream in my heart (Psalm 46:1–3).

A month later, the same lady who previously knocked at my door sent her friend to bring me to a doctor. She was concerned because my baby, who was supposed to be born on December 31, 1997, still had not been born. It was January 12, 1998. I was very scared. I didn't feel any movements or hiccups from the baby inside my womb. It felt as if a hard ball was inside me.

The doctor checked and he told me the bad news. "Your baby is dead. The umbilical cord is around his neck and there's no heartbeat. We have to rush you to the hospital to take the baby out."

I called my father who lived in that city and, trembling in fear, explained to him what the doctor just told me. I asked him to please take me to the hospital. I needed him so badly that day, not only to bring me to the hospital, but to be with me at that moment of despair. My father came, but he was too busy that day to stay with me, so he dropped me at the door of the hospital.

I was going into the elevator and I remember the suicide thoughts crossing my mind. The discouraging voices were saying, "You won't make it. You will die." (John 8:44). The nurse put in the IV and told me to relax. They were preparing the machine to operate on me in order to take the dead baby out. In that room, at that time, no one was there. Once more I found myself alone and hopeless, afraid and desperate for answers. But this time I was bold and serious about ending my life. I couldn't see any hope. I grabbed the IV and walked towards the window. I looked down and with a disconsolate cry I began looking for a way to open that window to jump and take my life (John 10:10).

I was confident that my brother would take good care of my oldest daughter and that this was best for me. I couldn't stop the pain and the struggles of life. But right then flashes of my dream with Jesus came to my mind, and that made me go back to the bed and rethink my decision. I cried with deep brokenness. Looking at the wall of the hospital, I asked Jesus, "If you ARE REAL, please show me now. Show me how real you are. Bring this baby back to life and I promise I will give you mine."

The minute I said that my baby jumped inside my womb. I knew that something just happened. I knew that LIFE just came back to my womb (Psalm 55:22). I screamed so loudly! The nurse came in and she called the doctor. He checked inside my womb and I could see the astonishment on their faces. The doctor told the nurse to break my water and she did. They pushed me in the hospital bed to the big machine, still thinking that surgery would be necessary. Very quickly they wrapped me with the blankets and with a rushing voice counted 1-2-3 and while they were passing me from the bed to the big machine, right there, my baby was born. The doctor caught him, cut the umbilical cord, checked him, and looked at me, saying, "Your baby is alive."

When I heard my baby boy cry, I knew in my heart that something different happened in my life that day. (Romans 8:38–39) If that wasn't enough, I experienced the presence of a God who was working in my heart in a strange and deeper way. Soon after the birth, five or more young men walked into the room. They were students from the university.

At that moment I felt heat in the left side of my head. It was as if someone was pulling my ear. I heard a voice tell me, "Say my name. Say who did this today." The strange thing is that I knew I wasn't supposed to say "God," but I was to say "JESUS."

Something deep in my heart knew that He was the one to whom I needed to give the glory and honor, so I screamed, "Jesus, thank you. Thank you, Jesus!" (Philippians 2:9). They all looked at me and started to laugh as if I was crazy. But I didn't care. I just knew that at that moment I was experiencing something that was out of the ordinary. That day, not only my unborn child was brought back to life, but I myself was back to life spiritually (1 Corinthians 2:11; Ephesians 2:1–10).

The next day it was time to leave, but I couldn't get out of the hospital because I had no money to pay the fees, and I had no one to take me home. My baby had no clothes to wear. I put him close to my body and wrapped him with my hospital garment. Finally, my sister came in, paid the fees, and brought my baby and me to my brother's house.

What I didn't know was that God had a plan. A month or two later my mom called to say that the American embassy gave her ten visas to bring all of her family to the USA. I know this does not happen often, so I believe it was the hand of God opening this door. It gave me so much hope. I thought this was an opportunity in my life to change, to be different. It was time for a new beginning in my life (Isaiah 43:19).

The day finally came. It was about six or seven months later, and I was sitting in a plane about to take off. I couldn't believe it. It was as if I had been lost and was finally found. It was like being rescued from a long, terrible time of suffering. I cried so hard on that plane! I sometimes think back to that feeling, that moment, and I have to confess that sometimes it is hard to believe how everything happened (Jeremiah 29:11).

I will never forget that day, that moment, when I heard a voice close behind me saying, "I am bringing you to this country so you can tell everyone that you get in contact with, that I AM REAL."

I looked back immediately and saw that no one was there. I have to admit that once again I thought I was losing my mind. I couldn't understand what was happening. Why was it that I heard voices, or saw prints on my bed, or felt a heat sensation that pulled my ear? (2 Samuel 22:14).

I kept everything in my heart. We finally arrived in America, and what a difference it was.

This country is blessed!

Chapter 1

My Cinderella Experience!

My mom lived in a predominantly immigrant area in New Jersey filled with older two-family houses. She rented the top floor of a house. Despite the cramped quarters, in my mind I thought she was rich! I compared her home here in the United States with our standard of living in Honduras. I did not understand why she never told us how rich she was. The first morning after I arrived in America, I looked outside the window to view my new neighborhood and I thought, "America is a rich country." Again, my first exposure to life in America consisted of living in a state-designated Urban Enterprise Zone that lowered the sales tax to encourage consumers to do business. Please forgive my ignorance, but I grew up stretching a pound of rice to feed a lot of people. But here we threw food away by the pound (Deuteronomy 28:8).

Months after coming to America, my mom found a job for my sister and me. It was time to help her with the financial load and take on our own responsibilities. There were two openings at the company–first and third shift. My mom decided that my sister would work first shift and I would work third shift. I was so upset about that decision. I thought my mom loved my sister more than she loved me. I walked to the agency every night while everybody was going to sleep. They offered a daily round-trip van service that brought me along, with other immigrant workers, to the manufacturing company the employment agency was in contract with. This was tough for me and very discouraging. My mental picture of the American dream and a rich America was collapsing. Reality was setting in. I was working hard, long overnight hours and had to pay taxes. I had to invest in the American system that I left my country of origin for. It became clear that to experience the American dream, I needed to work, and work hard. What I didn't know was that God had a plan for me (Jeremiah 29:11; Joshua 1:5).

You would think that, after all of the experiences I had before I came to this country, I would serve the Lord with all of my heart, right?

Not so fast ... instead, I continued living my sinful life. I got involved in a relationship with a married man and I got pregnant for the third time. A fool repeats his folly (2 Peter 2:22).

I told that man about my pregnancy. There was little to discuss as he brought me to an abortion clinic to eliminate what, for us, was a "problem." He wanted the pleasure, but not the responsibility of his own actions. To say the least, my relationships with men were consistent and predictable–rejection, pain, and another wound that would cause an emotional scar.

I remember riding in his car on our way to Union City, New Jersey. He held my hand so tightly as he tried to encourage me and make me understand that this was best. But something inside was cutting my heart like a knife. The feeling would not let me go. I went through this before and I was bold enough to keep my babies, but this time, I couldn't go back to my mom's house with another "problem" pregnancy. I came to America to change, to be different, to make different choices–better choices. What happened? Why was I once again trapped by these circumstances? Why? (James 4:4; Ephesians 5:3; 5:11–12; Colossians 3:5).

I went inside the clinic as the father of my unborn child was talking to the lady at the front desk. They called my name right away and brought me inside a room. I remember walking through the hallway and seeing many women, both young and old. One thing I can say is, not one of them looked happy or excited about their decision. Everyone looked concerned, sad, terrified, and in shame, as we all knew that this wasn't the right thing to do. I was trembling in fear while preparing for the procedure. A nurse abruptly interrupted the doctor and he left the room. The nurse said to me, "You will have to come back, the doctor said the baby is too small. We need to let it grow and then we'll do it." What an opportunity I had to rethink my decision, but instead I found a way to continue our plan (Matthew 15:19; Psalm 55:23; Proverbs 12:2; John 8:44).

I came out and the father of my unborn child told me, "They couldn't do it because I don't have enough cash. I don't want to use a credit card." That's when I realized that the problem wasn't that the baby was too small as the nurse told me. It was the amount of money that was too small, so I offered to pay the rest out of my own pocket. He went back in with my payment and completed the financial transaction to end the life of my child (2 Timothy 3:2).

The nurse called me back and the abortionist performed the life-terminating procedure. It was done quickly. They gave him a prescription and we went right away to the pharmacy. He came back with the medicine and flowers. I remember asking him, "Who are those flowers for? For me or for the baby we just killed?" He just laughed.

On our way to my mom's house, I was devastated inside and very confused. I was screaming in my heart. I don't know what hurt most–the physical pain or the pain in my heart because of the knowledge of what I just did (Psalm 139:13–16; Jeremiah 1:5; Isaiah 64:8; Deuteronomy 30:19).

I remember thinking, "Before I didn't know better, but now I do know better." I couldn't understand myself. Why would I continue living this type of life? Why couldn't I change? I was not in Honduras and the people around me were different, so I could not blame anybody other than myself. I began to realize that the problem of my wrong decisions was not the place or the people–it was me. It was my heart and my heart's desires (1 Samuel 16:7).

As I arrived at my mother's house, I acted as if everything was normal. I put on the mask of happiness and continued life as normal, but deep inside my heart, I was hiding the pain, guilt, shame, and condemnation. That day I asked that man to never come to my door or near me again. He laughed as if he did not believe that this was the end of our relationship, but it was.

This abortion became a painful secret for me. It brought shame and sorrow, but I couldn't talk about it. I buried it deep with all of the other roots that already existed in my heart. I easily hid this from every eye that saw me, except from the eyes of God. He delivered me in a supernatural way from this tormented pain (Psalm 46:1).

That same day of the abortion, I was crying in my room. I began to talk to God. I asked, "God, why? Why? Please tell me, why can't I change?" I felt as if I wanted to reach into my heart and rip it out of my chest. That's how disappointed I was. I continued crying, asking God for help, "Please help me. Please change me. God, I am your vessel, please break me in pieces and glue me back together again. Paint my soul with the colors of your blood." I cried until I had no more words. I threw myself on the floor and I felt this brokenness inside like never before. I began to surrender my life to God and right there I heard, "You don't know me. There's more." I felt as if someone just turned my head to the side and there it was … what I was missing. The living water that washed my soul and cleansed my heart … the Bible. How did I not think of it before? Why did this never come to my mind? (Hebrews 4:12).

Immediately, I knew that in this collection of books were all of my answers. I grabbed it and began to read it as if hope was back. I would go to work, but I could not wait to get home to read. I wanted more and more. I wanted to know who this Jesus was who raised my son back to life and spoke to me many times. I continued reading, and the more I read, the more I knew and the more I wanted Him. I began to recognize Him, His voice, His presence, His power, His forgiveness, and overall, His love for me (Romans 5:8).

This was when my prayer life began. I entered into a relationship with the true and only God, my Father, the one who created me. The one who knew me and formed me in my mother's womb (Psalm 139:13–14).

I discovered that He is the I AM and that He is REAL, and that He works miracles. I entered into a relationship with Jesus. He is the one who spoke to me, and the one who sat on my bed the whole night. We became friends. I discovered that whatever I asked in His name, He would give it to me (John 14:13).

My first request was, "Give me a husband. Give me a man who will worship you. A man who will put your desires before his own." While asking for this, I saw a picture of my family in my imagination, a godly family that had God as the center of our home. I don't believe this was a coincidence, but at that moment I heard a noise. I looked at the window and there was a dove (Luke 3:22). Immediately, I thought this must be the Holy Spirit saying to me, "It's done!" so I believed (Matthew 9:29).

I continued working at the same third-shift job my mom found for me. The hours were difficult enough, but I also had to deal with personalities that were more challenging. Specifically, I had a lot of issues with a supervisor. We could not get along. For some reason, I could not find favor in her eyes. She made me feel very insignificant. She made jokes in English about me and laughed

with other employees who understood her humorous cracks at my expense. One of her friends who also worked at the company partnered with her to make me look foolish by asking me questions in English. Because I could not understand what he was saying, he would point his finger and laugh at the expression on my confused face. I had to routinely hold back my tears of embarrassment.
I felt obligated to stay there and take it, because there were a lot of Spanish-speaking people. At that time, I did not speak English beyond the few dozen words needed to communicate in a factory. What I did not know was that one day, God would use all of these people, particularly that one supervisor, to bring me to the place where He wanted me. All things work together for our own good (Romans 8:28).

In a moment that would eventually change my life, that Hispanic supervisor asked me to pick up some crushed, flattened boxes and bring them to the warehouse for recycling. I honestly felt humiliated. There were men that she could ask, but instead she asked me. When I was walking toward the warehouse, carrying those boxes, she was laughing with other workers because she was humiliating me. I walked with a knot in my throat, crying and thinking, "Why do I have to go through this? Why do things never change for me?"

It was here that I felt like the Israelites after God took them out of Egypt–their place of bondage–in a miraculous way. In their wilderness wandering when things started to get a little bit hard, they wanted to go back to Egypt. They started to complain and grumble against God. I have to admit that I did the same. "It was better in Honduras; I want to go back." Let's be clear, there was no way my situation was better in Honduras! However, I was not expecting to experience this kind of humiliation here. Once again, life would present hard circumstances that would require me to persevere and endure everything that came my way, even when I felt mocked or humiliated. But God saw my affliction (Exodus 3:7–9).

What I did not know was that in that moment I was walking, step by step, into my destiny. His plans are always better than mine (Isaiah 55:8–9). If God can use a rock to bring forth water for the Israelites to drink, He truly can use an immature supervisor to bring me into my destiny (Exodus 17).

The first time I entered the company's warehouse, I saw a man sitting inside a glass office, working on his computer. I got closer and closer when, suddenly, I dropped the boxes. The loud noise made that man look up, and there we were, looking at each other as if we both were waiting for that moment. I can only explain what I felt inside my heart. I walked back to the production line, but all that I could remember was our eyes being separated by the walls. I could not stop thinking about that man. I even asked my coworker if she knew who that man was. I described what he looked like and she answered, "Stop looking at those men. They don't care about us. They're all married." (Isaiah 41:10).

Minutes later, I heard a voice that made everything on the inside of me pause. Yes, it was him, the same man, asking for my name. For a moment I even forgot my name. I could not believe that this was happening. I told him my name and he left. The look in his eyes and the smile on his face told me the truth. I knew that he did not need my name for any other reason than his own interest (Psalm 143:8). I continued telling my coworker that that was the man I saw, the man I was asking her for. She responded, "Glennys, you're trying to reach the stars." (Ephesians 4:2).

Why is it that some women think so low of themselves? I was confused about her comment. Was it because I was a Hispanic woman who could not speak English? Why was I feeling like a small fish in a big pond? I knew that I came to America to change, to be different, to live my dreams. I was not going to stay the way I was. I had no reason not to go to school, learn English, get a better job, and be somebody. I thought about the events that led to this moment. I came from Honduras legally. Yes, with God all things are possible (Matthew 19:26). My brothers, sisters, nieces, and my children, all waited in line to come to this country. My mom paid the money, and one day, after many years of waiting and living without our own mother, the American Embassy gave my mom ten visas to bring all of her family to America (Deuteronomy 10:21; Jeremiah 32:27). I am extremely thankful for this.

I had experienced the blessing of being an immigrant entering into this amazing country the right way–the legal way (Romans 13:1–7). I love America and I came to stay, to serve, and to swear my allegiance to it. However, I never went to school to learn English. My faith was growing and growing. I started to believe in a God of the impossible. I asked Him to teach me this beautiful language. "God, all languages are yours, please anoint my tongue and put that language in my mouth," I asked. I have to admit that I was confused about the "speaking in tongues" the Bible talks about. I thought it meant English, Spanish, etc. (Mark 16:17).

I bought myself an English and Spanish Bible. I started teaching myself to speak English and it worked for me because I believed in my heart that it would. God was honoring my faith, as misinformed as it was. While reading my Bible, I was also learning the language. Meanwhile, I continued working in the same place. Every day I walked through those doors, and there was that man from the warehouse with a big smile waiting for me just to say "hello." This went on for months. Every night on my way to work in the agency's van, I would think of how to say something more than just "hello". I practiced the entire way there, but for some reason, when the moment came, I couldn't say anything. I could not understand what was happening. Why does this man make me feel in a way I never felt? (Philippians 4:6–7).

One day, he finally asked to sit at my table and have lunch with me. We started to eat together almost every day around 3 a.m. during our midnight shift break time. It was here when things started to quickly progress. We started to date and get to know each other more. He came to my house and met my family, and everyone loved him. What I found very strange was how respectful he was, he barely even touched my hand. This type of relationship was strange to me. We continued working together and little did I know, he eventually became my supervisor. Our relationship grew deeper and deeper, or I should say, better and better, until one day when he came to me and said, "Tonight is the last night you can work here. Just finish the shift and I'll call the agency, so they don't send you here anymore" (John 14:26).

Yes, he fired me! Honestly, I could not understand what was happening. He talked to me about it before and he thought we were in agreement, but unfortunately, because I did not speak the language yet, I did not fully understand him. There were some coworkers spreading negative rumors about me because he was my supervisor. He did not want my reputation to be ruined knowing that our relationship was becoming more serious. After all, if we needed to choose which one of us had to leave, that would be me because I was a temporary employee. They could send me somewhere else, but he was the salaried supervisor. We would need that income in our future, he thought (Ephesians 5:15–16).

Everything he told me, even that he was going to fire me, I just responded with, "OK," though I did not really understand him. We communicated with my little English, his little Spanish, and our own "sign" language. God's grace is sufficient (2 Corinthians 12:9). What's impossible for Him? However, not understanding my supposedly agreed upon employment termination plan, I became very angry! I left the company the moment he fired me. I was so confused, thinking that everything was over, including our relationship. It was surprising to him because he thought we agreed to it (1 Corinthians 14:33).

Early the next morning, I was praying, and I really felt the need to call him. He had just got home the moment of my phone call and, with my broken English, I asked, "Can you come back here so we can talk?" He responded, "Yes, I'll be there in an hour." Despite just driving an hour home, he did not hesitate to make the return commute. This was the first time I understood him clearly when he said, "I want you to be my wife. I want to marry you." (Ecclesiastes 4:9).

After that day, we became more serious about our relationship and our plan to get married. During this time, I found another job in a hotel as a housekeeper cleaning rooms. After a very stressful day, as I was walking out with other ladies, I saw a beautiful bouquet of flowers on top of the counter at the front desk that really called all of our attention. I immediately wished it was for me, but I thought that maybe it was for one of the beautiful female supervisors that work there. While all of us were passing by the front desk, a man called me and pointed at the bouquet of flowers and said, "This is for you." I was very surprised, almost in shock. I could not believe it. My heart jumped with joy. I looked at everybody and felt humble to be the chosen one. I walked out of the job all dirty and sweaty but holding my beautiful bouquet. To my surprise, he was standing outside waiting for me to bring me home.

I have to admit that I never had the honor and the privilege to experience such a pure love. We got home and right in front of my house was a limousine. Immediately, the thought of "I wish it was for me," crossed my mind, but at the same time, I rejected the idea that something like that could happen to me. Again, I never experienced this, no one ever treated me this way and It was hard to even expect it.

I was getting out of the car as he grabbed my hand and said, "Go get ready and when you are done, I'll be waiting for you in that limousine to take you out to New York City." I still did not believe it and I laughed at him, thinking he was joking. I said, "Yeah, right," and went inside the house. I walked in thinking, "What if this is true?" I walked into the living room and my mom was at the window, looking more nervous than I was, and she said, "Daughter, go get ready, that limousine is for you." And that's when I believed it. I looked through the window and he was at the door of the limousine waving. "Oh my gosh, what do I do?" I thought, and I started to feel more nervous. I walked into my room and my sisters were there, waiting for me to help me get ready, and that's when I woke up into my reality that something special was happening. Something I never experienced and never expected–a real man who did not see my past, but instead he saw my future! Finally, I came out and by my sister's choice I wore a long red dress that really made me feel that special moment of my life–a Cinderella moment that every woman with a past like mine will love to experience with her prince (Psalm 37:23–24; Deuteronomy 28:1–14).

Like Cinderella, after I was abused, mistreated, rejected, and hurt–here I had a man who respected me, cared for me, and wanted to make me his wife. Sometimes it was so hard for me to understand. I never experienced a clean and pure relationship. This was a man who would take me out for dinner and bring me back home. This ideal relationship was not normal for me. Let me remind you that I was a single mother of two, and he was bringing me teddy bears, flowers, trips in a limousine, and, finally, to the altar. Eyes have never seen, and ears have never heard what God has for us–his children (1 Corinthians 2:9).

He not only built a relationship with me, but also with my two children. He became their father the moment they saw each other for the first time (1 Corinthians 13:13; Ephesians 4:2–3).

I found out later that this man sent my father in Honduras a letter asking for my hand and went to look for my mother at her job to ask her permission to marry me (Galatians 6:9). On February 14th, 2000, he took me out for dinner in a beautiful restaurant overlooking the bay. There was a piano player by my side and a bouquet of roses placed on the center of the table. He nervously bent down on one knee with the ring in his hand and asked me, "Will you marry me?" (1 Peter 5:6-7) I couldn't believe what I was living at that moment. Of course, my response was "Yes!"

I could not wait to go back home to my mother's house that night. When I got there, my mom was sitting in the living room and I screamed, "I'm getting married. I'm getting married!" as I showed her my ring. She had a big smile on her face, and she thanked God for it. I woke my sisters up and showed it to them also. I literally thought I was living in a dream. Truly, God makes a way where there is no way (Isaiah 43:19)!

On May 19, 2000, we were saying "I do." (Isaiah 41:10; Mark 10:9; Jeremiah 1:12) But the night before the wedding, I had my John the Baptist moment. "Is this the one?" After I saw everything and experienced everything, doubt came in. I asked myself, "Is he the one that I should marry?"

I was feeling like John the Baptist when he was behind bars. After he declared to the whole world that Jesus was the one, when things started to get serious and persecution came, he sent his disciples to ask Jesus if He was the one (Luke 7:18–19). It was the same with me. I knew that Shawn was the man God sent to find me and to be his wife, but when things started to get serious and I was about to make a lifetime commitment, doubt showed up. Is this the one? What if he is not? Isn't he too tall and too white? Yes, even those things crossed my mind because I never thought that one day I would marry a man who was so different from me (Isaiah 55:8).

I thank God I made the right choice. For the first time in my life, I decided to make a decision contrary to my emotions and my feelings. I knew that deep in my heart I was doing it because in the eyes of God this was the right thing to do. We had a very simple wedding and honeymoon. We needed to get back to our role of being parents of two children (Numbers 23:19).

Here is where our real life began.

R eview–Coming to America gave me hope that my life was going to change, but my expectations were in the wrong place. Months later, I was in an abortion clinic ending the life of my child as a result of my sinful desires. It was not the place or the people who were the problem for my life to be different. It was my own heart.

E ncouragement–Be transformed by the renewing of your mind, reading the Word of God each day. Regardless of the circumstances life presents, you must persevere and endure because God has a hope and a future for all of us. Don't make decisions based upon your emotions, always pursue God's will, no matter if your flesh desires something else.

A pply–Romans 12:1–21; Ezekiel 36:26; Psalm 51:10; 1 Peter 2:1–25; Proverbs 4:23; Ephesians 4:22–24; Luke 6:43–45; 1 Peter 1:16–17; Proverbs 27:19; Mark 12:30; Matthew 7:21; 2 Corinthians 5:17; Deuteronomy 30:19.

L earned–The state of my current situation does not determine my destiny. Regardless of my humiliation, I kept trusting in God and it was Him who changed my life forever. He gave me a husband who loves me with all of his heart. He makes all things new.

Chapter 2

My Controlling Power Experience!

Our journey together began. We were now husband and wife. I had no framework or point of reference to know how to have a successful marriage or even what a successful marriage is supposed to be. I was clueless on how relationships work. I only had experience on how they did not work. First, I refused to accept the idea that I needed to submit to my prince (Ephesians 5:22). Submission was not my cup of tea. And let someone tell me what to do? In Spanish we say, "Hay Dios mio!" ("OH MY GOD!")

I remember one time the flour tortillas flew across the kitchen as our argument got out of control. Then there was the challenge of learning each other's languages. I found his *Learn Spanish* book in the garbage, and self-teaching myself English stopped. I was still reading my Bible and spending time with God, but I found a Spanish-speaking church that my husband did not attend because he could not understand the language. Things were changing; now it was him who was being forced to learn my language and follow my decisions. At that point, none of this made sense, so I began to create my own story in my head. I believed that he did not want to go to church. He wasn't really a Christian, he just acted like one to marry me.

My assumptions were, of course, completely wrong. If he came home early or late from work, we would fight. If there was money or no money, we would fight. I would go to church and lie to the pastor and members of the church about my husband, saying that he abused me, and that he was this terrible man, only because he did not submit to me. Things were not going the way I wanted (1 Timothy 3:11; Proverbs 12:4; 14:1; 25:24).

The jealousy in me began to work its way out (James 3:14; 16; 1 Corinthians 3:3). I thought the worst of my husband. What went wrong? My Cinderella story was changing. I was confused. I told some people the story of how God brought us together, and to others, the story of the terrible husband that I had. Honestly, my little Spanish church was not helping. Every time I went to a service, I learned more and more about religious legalism. What impacted my life the most (in a negative way) was that almost everything was blamed on demons and evil (Colossians 2:8; Galatians 2:21; Matthew 23:23–28).

Please don't take me wrong, I believe there is evil in this world and the Bible clearly tells us about the work of the enemy, but it messes up a Christian's mind and creates a spiritual imbalance when they walk around casting out demons that do not exist. They start to live a life that is restrictive. There is no joy and no peace because everything is evil. This sometimes makes Christians feel like they are the only perfect humans in the world. This is not spiritually healthy. This kind of teaching makes people walk in their emotions at all times, always looking out for the non-existent "demons" in others (Matthew 7:5).

This unhealthy teaching manifested in a crazy way. I didn't even know how to dress anymore. I thought that I needed to wear certain types of clothes. This was difficult for me because I hated skirts, but I felt obligated to wear them. I was trying to follow the example of all the women leaders in the church and their "protocols". One day, I came home from church and I threw away my children's favorite toys and brand-new sets of blankets because the pastor said that that specific cartoon was created to worship demons. What is so funny is that that same day, I looked through my window and saw a lady taking everything I just threw away in the dumpsters. She was jumping up and down with her blessing– my children's toys and blankets. I personally believe that some people give Satan credit for their own mistakes because of their own wrong decisions in life (Ephesians 2:1–22).

My emotions were all mixed up. Not only did I believe that everything was evil, but my anger and jealousy grew more intense and uncontrollable. One time, my husband came a few minutes late from work. He walked into the kitchen, and I saw something on his light blue shirt. In my mind, I thought that was evidence of all my assumptions–a long blond hair. I grabbed it! I was going to put it in a Ziploc bag, just to show the court the evidence. You might be thinking that I was going crazy, and yes, I was (1 Timothy 6:4).

Nothing was satisfying me. However, I kept reading my Bible and seeking God's presence. I would go to church and, because my husband did not go with me, we would fight when I came back. I was convinced that I was doing the right thing, that I was the super-spiritual one. I thought that it was my husband who was the wrong one; the one who did not want to obey God and submit–to me. He needed to change. Let me remind you that at the time we were dating, he had his own house, and he attended a church, but when we got married, I decided for us to live in a town far away from his house because I wanted to live close to my mother and the rest of my family. I found the Hispanic church for us to attend. I was living a life totally contrary to the Word, and the people in my church believed me and stood with me. No one ever told me the hard, uncomfortable truth of how wrong I was. They were convinced that my tears and my story were telling them the truth, and because they didn't see my husband attending church, they believed me even more and were careless about his part of the story (Romans 16:17–18; James 1:26; Exodus 20:16).

Since the beginning of our marriage, I was the one making decisions, so when my husband had enough and tried to turn things around, it was too late, I thought he changed. He did not love me. I believed that he was terrible because he did not let me run the house anymore. God have mercy! (1 Corinthians 14:33).

Many times I saw my husband crying and that bothered me even more. I thought something was wrong with him. I wondered why he did not fight back. I mistreated and disrespected him at all times. I did not trust him or his abilities. I thought I was the one who needed to rule the house because, in my eyes, I was the stronger one, and the one who prayed. I never saw him praying or going to church. Even the way he took care of our two children bothered me. I thought he was being a hypocrite. When they did something wrong, he would sit with them and open the Bible and show them what the Word says about that specific situation, but my way to discipline my children was different. Therefore, in my mind, my husband was wrong even in this. I never saw or experienced a man full of love, kindness, and compassion. This was strange to me and very uncomfortable. I was used to living life in a different way where chaos, abuse, and friction was normal. A gentle and quiet spirit in a husband by my side made me nervous. I thought that if he did not yell and verbally abuse me, then he didn't know how to fight in life (Proverbs 21:9; 14:1; 1 Timothy 5:6).

I continued reading my Bible and found out that God sees my heart, and therefore, I began to see my own heart. I tried to put the Scriptures I read into practice, but in my own way. (1 Samuel 16:7) I realized that I was hurt, and hurt people hurt people. I started to feel the brokenness of my heart. Even though my prayer life got deeper and deeper and I had long conversations with the Lord, asking Him to help me, to change me, and to change my heart, I could not let go of my anger, my power, my own way of thinking, and my unforgiveness (Psalm 51:10).

My struggle continued. I know some people refuse to talk about their past, but for me, I needed to go back to my past and pull out all the roots that were deep in my heart. They were not only affecting my marriage, but my relationship with God. I did not know how to receive His care and protection, or how to accept Him (God) as my only security and Identity (John 1:12). To move forward in my walk with God, I needed a circumcision of my own heart (Romans 2:25–29).

It was hard for me to rest my mind and soul in the peace of God because of my past. I did not know how to let go of trying to survive on my own. I was afraid of my future without my own controlling power. I had a man who wanted to do life with me and wanted to protect me and help me to find my identity. Yet, it was hard because, just like the Israelites when they came out of Egypt, they complained and wanted to go back to Egypt. That was all they knew. Being in bondage was their security (Exodus 14). I only knew how to live as an orphan, and to become "fatherless no more and a child of God" was very difficult for me. I simply did not know how to trust, how to be taken care of, or how to be loved. It was like fighting a long war and then, after winning and getting the victory, you do not even know how to celebrate. I was so used to fighting, and fighting alone in life, that it became my identity. Giving up on what I knew to do the best felt as if I was giving up on life. I built up walls of insecurity to protect myself. I did not trust anyone. I believed that no one loved me; no one cared. I was living with no rules, no authority, no purpose, and no God (Ephesians 1:5).

My poor heart was like a treasure box where everything was collected (Revelation 21:4). I needed a "deep root pulling" healing power. How could I love my husband the way God wanted me to love him, with respect and honor, (1 Peter 3:1; Ephesians 5:22), when I did not know real love–Christ's love? Instead, I was giving my husband what I had and what I knew how to give–anger and rejection (2 Corinthians 12:9; Psalm 139:23–24).

I had a contaminated heart. (Proverbs 4:23) I was completely blinded. This was not only contaminating and blinding me, but it was affecting my children also. Unforgiveness is like a skunk that sprays its repulsive stench on everyone around it. Many times, I heard my own words of anger coming out of their little mouths. Again, I could not give what I did not have, and what I had I gave to everyone around me–anger and rejection. Even though I knew the truth that could set me free, I chose to hold onto my own prison, and the longer it took for me to come out of this bondage, the longer it took for me to experience the goodness of God that brought me to repentance (Luke 6:45; James 1:22; Romans 2:4).

My long conversations with Jesus, my Bible reading and praying continued. I wish I could say that instantly I was changed, but that did not happen. It took several years for me to really walk in the righteous path of God and to be the wife He wanted me to be. Meanwhile, my husband was very patient with me and continued loving and serving me. He understood that a person can never change another person's heart, but God can if we allow it. It took time for the Word of God to heal my heart and the Holy Spirit to train, change, and transform my mind. It was not easy. Not because the Word has no power, it was because I rejected it. I could not accept that I was wrong, that I had been wrong all those years of my life. I chose to hold onto my own thinking. Change is something that you have to want. You have to die to your own way of thinking, to your own desires, and to your own flesh (Galatians 5:17; 2 Peter 1:6–8).

As I was going through this process of change, I read Malachi 3:10, and it caught my attention. It was as if God was challenging me to test Him. I came with the idea to bring a big check to the church to cover all the tithes that we never paid from the time we got married. I talked to Shawn about it and he agreed with me. That day, early in the morning, I was on my way to the church, with my two children in the car, when suddenly a car came out of nowhere as I tried to change lanes, but it was too late. I lost control on a one way, heavily traveled highway. I crossed all the lanes and was about to hit the overpass guardrails. I screamed as loud as I could, "Jesus, Jesus!" Somehow, my car suddenly turned. I felt as if someone moved my foot and hit the brake pedal to make the car stop. I ended up in the opposite direction and I did not know what to do. The only damage was a badly scratched passenger side door. Thankfully, a man came to my window. I opened it and he looked at me and my children and said, "You are OK. Your children are OK. The car can get replaced. Get out." He looked like someone who was in authority and on a mission–a very important mission. I obeyed him. I got out of the car and he turned it around in the right direction. As he came out of the car, he said to me, "Go and do what you need to do quickly." I got in the car and before I took off, I looked out my window to say thank you, but he was gone. I looked everywhere and he was completely gone (Colossians 1:16).

I went to the church and gave the pastor our tithe, and then I drove to a friend's house. She could not believe how I came out of that accident with just a bad scratch all over the passenger side of my car. We both knew that the road was a very busy road. There is no way all of this could happen without hitting another car or getting hit by one. Also, what was that man doing there and how did he know that I was going to do something very important that day? I have no other explanation than to believe that it was an angel sent by God (Psalm 91:11).

I believe that this decision to pay our tithes and give God what belongs to Him has a lot to do with all of our blessings–financially, spiritually, physically, mentally, and what helped to change our marriage. We have paid our tithes to the Lord since then, and God has thrown open the floodgates of heaven and poured out so much blessing that there is not room enough to contain it. He is a promise keeper (Numbers 23:19).

Another time God protected me from dying was a day I was coming home from a store. I missed the warning lights and

the alarms of an oncoming train. I was deep in my thoughts as
I crossed a train track. The loud horn of the train made me look
fast to my right. The train was just feet away from me. I pushed the
gas and in a miraculous way I was on the other side. I could see
through my mirror the train passing right behind me. My heart was
beating so fast! I started to cry and thank God for His protection.
He is always watching over us (Psalm 46:1; Psalm 121:5–8).

These experiences helped me to pay more attention to my Father
in Heaven and to understand that He loves and cares for me. They
helped me to be more aware of His protection and that He has
plans for me here on earth.

We finally moved to a different apartment, close to the church my
husband attended before we got married. It was there that I started
my baby steps of submission, not only to my husband, but to the
authority of the Word of God (James 4:7). The same pastor that
God used in my husband's life years before, God used in my life
to help me grow spiritually. I could not wait to be in church and
I started to volunteer there. I even worked in the church's daycare
during the week. The fire in our bones to do things together for
the kingdom of God started there. Everything was different. We
attended this church together as a family, and it was there where
I found out more about my husband's life. Church members would
tell me stories of the things he did before we met. He loved this
church so much and everyone talked of him as a man after the
heart of God. They told me how he used to preach the gospel, clean
up the bathrooms of the church, and separate the garbage for the
recycling truck (Colossians 3:12; 23–24; Matthew 20:26).

I started to know my husband's heart. His passion for bringing
souls to the kingdom of God inspired me. I was in awe of the kind
of man I had by my side. Sometimes I thought, "Who is this man
and what did I do to deserve such love?" What was so amazing to
me was that the same thing that was happening in my relationship
with my husband, was happening in my relationship with God.

The scales were falling from my eyes (Acts 9:18; Psalm 119:37). Things were turning around. I was not only falling in love with my husband, but I was falling in love with my Lord and Savior–Jesus Christ. I started to realize that Shawn was truly a man sent by God to find me.

One day we had a prayer meeting and something amazing happened to me. The pastor's wife and some church members (including my husband) were praying and speaking in tongues. I was sitting quietly when, all of a sudden, I felt the presence of God. My lips started to move very quickly making some unknown sounds. I was so nervous but excited at the same time. I knew that what was happening was what the Bible talks about on the day of Pentecost. (Acts 2:1–4). I got my husband's attention and told him what had just happened. We were both extremely happy and excited about my experience. No one touched me. No one trained me or anointed my tongue at that moment. The Holy Spirit just came upon me and I have been speaking in tongues ever since. This is powerful. When I do not know what to pray for, or when I find myself in situations that I do not know what to do, I just speak in tongues because I believe that is how my spirit connects with the Spirit of God. I have seen things move immediately (John 14:16; Acts 1:8)!

We started our evangelism work together as a family. We represented our church by standing at the door of Walmart, with their permission, to share Christ and offer tracts to passing shoppers. At some recreational parks, we would give things away and talk to people about Christ and His salvation. Many people received Jesus as their Lord and Savior. I was determined not to miss an opportunity to bring souls to the kingdom of God. I knew in my heart that this was my mission here on earth. As I said before, people only give what they have. Salvation was changing my life, so I wanted everyone around me to know that this is the answer. I was feeling like the woman who found her lost coin. I wanted the whole world to know that I found what was missing in my heart–Jesus Christ (Luke 15:8–10).

I can also relate to the Samaritan woman at the moment she was found by her Messiah at the well, and He began to tell her things from her past that she was hiding. Her sin bound her in misery, as she was living with shame. But the light shined so bright on her that day and opened her eyes to understanding as she recognized Jesus as the Son of God. She ran to tell everyone about Him because in Him she found what was missing–life (John 4)!

One morning, I woke up screaming and trembling in fear with terrible heart palpitations because of a dream. In my dream, I came out of my house and looked up to the sky. It was dark as if black smoke were covering it. People from the entire world could see it. I was so nervous because I never saw the sky turning that dark during the day. Suddenly, I heard someone scream, "It's Jesus!" and at the same time the sky cracked open, and a shining, bright light was coming out. It was getting brighter and brighter, covering the darkness. I saw Jesus coming down. His clothes were white, extremely bright, and He had His arms open. Behind him were thousands of angels, dressed in white shining a brilliant light, and each of these angels were carrying a candle in their hands. When Jesus touched the ground, something happened immediately. I ran to Him crying and screaming, "No, please, no. Jesus, please go back. Not now. People are not ready. Please Jesus, not now." I was crying out for the souls that did not receive Jesus as their Lord and Savior yet, but it was too late. I got close to Him and I cannot explain what happened. When I saw His face, I fell down on the ground almost dead. I could not talk. I could not move. I was like a dry leaf in His presence. My heart stopped. My mind was unconscious. His face was too powerful for any human beings to behold. Then I woke up in my dream and got up from the ground. I looked around at a terrifying scene. The whole world looked as if there had just been a war. There was chaos everywhere, and everything was permitted. I saw people at the door of many houses relaxing, laughing, and partying. People were even sitting on top of cars, having fun. There was no sense of urgency. No rules. No laws. I walked around with an inexplicable feeling in my heart knowing that I stayed, too. I did not go with Jesus, as many other people did. I walked inside my house looking for my Bible and discovered my family and my Bible were gone. I could not find that pink Women's Bible that I was looking for. The desperation in my heart grew intense. I was confused by everything. The disaster in the world was breathtaking, but people did not look concerned. Instead, they were enjoying their life as normal. The only exception was those who, like me, were "Christians", but stayed behind. I even recognized a man who is a pastor who also stayed behind. He looked extremely sad and distressed. The pain in my chest was unbearable. I cried so deep and loud. In silence, I was begging Jesus to help me, to take me out of there. Somehow, I knew that there was no way I was going to get help, and that was even more painful. Suddenly, my human mind and heart could not take it anymore, and my conscience began to react saying, "This is not real, this will never happen to me. This is a dream. It has to be a dream; wake up–wake up!" Right then, I heard a voice that said, "I put you in the feet of those who will stay behind, so you would know what they will feel." Finally, I woke up screaming for help.

My husband comforted and encouraged me. I have to admit that the feeling in my heart left months later. I talked to my pastor and I told him my dream. It is rare for me to share this dream with anybody, unless I know God wants me to do so. I know that my dream was just a dream, not exactly how the Bible warns us about the second coming of the groom (Jesus) to pick up His bride (the Church), but for me it was a way of ministering to my heart. It gave me compassion and grace for those who do not know Jesus as their Lord and Savior. Sharing this dream encourages Christians to keep watching and praying because no one knows the day or the hour. Salvation is real and every human being on the planet needs it. This is why Jesus died on the cross. I will stay in eternal suffering without Him, as in my dream, crying for help but knowing that I will never get it. I believe this explains more about my passion for souls and drives me to do more for the kingdom of God (Proverbs 11:30).

I was being molded more and more. My experiences with God were getting deeper and deeper. What really amazes me is that my obedience opened the gate of many blessings (1 Samuel 15:22). I was obedient to follow my husband and move back to his neighborhood and attend his church. This helped me tremendously to improve my English pronunciation because we lived among English-speaking people. I entered my husband's culture, or I should say, "America's culture." God is a perfect God, and He knew that I needed this. As a wife, I needed to submit to my husband, and as an immigrant I needed to persevere. I needed to speak the language and work hard because nothing is free. Everything has a cost, including government assistance, and if I'm not the one paying for it, then someone else is. Even in this, God changed my way of thinking. He is the truth that sets me free (John 8:31–32).

One thing about God is that He does not miss anything. He knows everything we are dealing with. Something that really was bothering me was my relationship with my oldest daughter. She was the one who suffered the most because of my wrong and selfish decisions in years past. I knew that I loved her, but for some reason I could not give her affection, probably because I did not know how. I took care of all her physical needs of course, but there was no relationship or bond between us. I knew she loved me, and I could see in her little facial expressions the hunger for her mom's affection, but I could not do it. How could I give what I never had? (2 Corinthians 8:12).

I was on my way to a women's retreat from our church, and I began to think about what would happen if we got into an accident and I was to die. Immediately, I began to fight those thoughts, but something deeper in my heart (I believe it was the Holy Spirit) said, "What would happen to your daughter? She never experienced her mother's affection." And right there, I began to cry and asked God to please give me another chance. I promised Him that I was going to fix my relationship with my daughter.

I knew deep in my heart that I did not want her to live the same life I lived (Proverbs 22:6).

The retreat was amazing. It helped me to understand what I needed to do, what I was commanded to do, with my daughter's situation. I went back home and the first thing I did was sit my daughter on my lap and grabbed her as my baby. With tears running down my cheeks, I asked her to forgive me, "Forgive me for not being the mother I needed to be. Forgive me for not responding to your affection. Forgive me for not giving you attention." I promised her that from that moment on I was going to be the mother that God wanted me to be for her. I hugged and kissed her in a way I never did before. We became friends and have been close since then. Sometimes we have to do what God commanded us to do, regardless of what we feel. I needed to stop thinking about myself, my pain, and what I went through in my own childhood, but think of others, in this case, my daughter. I needed to break the curse, so it does not go from generation to generation, but instead ceases under my watch. She was growing too quickly and not having her mother's love, affection, and attention could affect her life forever as it did mine. After I obeyed God, I realized that my affection for her was there, deep in my heart, wrapped in an unconditional love. Any woman can be a mother by giving birth, but parenting you have to learn. It is not just buying things and taking care of your child physically, but emotionally, and, the most important, spiritually. We need to teach, guide, and protect them with love, care, and affection. God is the Author of Love and He wants us to love and forgive the way He loves and forgive us. All of this was happening so quickly. God was transforming my heart and teaching me to live life His way. I was learning to be a mother, a wife, and, above all, to be a child of God (1 John 4:16).

Our journey and experiences with the Lord continued. Finally, after being married for a few years, I opened some of my husband's boxes. I found a video of a great well-known preacher, which was amazing to me because one time in a group conversation in my

Spanish church, his name was mentioned as a man who preaches the Word. To find his video in my own home was very interesting to me. I put on this VHS tape. I might not have understood much English, but let me tell you, I understood every word that man was preaching. It was so powerful that I could feel the presence of God in my living room. It was that day that I heard, "As I called my son Abraham to leave everything and go, I'm calling you today" (Genesis 12:1).

That same night, my husband came home from work with the mail in his hand. Among the mail was a letter from who do you think? Yes, that same preacher's ministry invited my husband to go to their partners' weekend. I was astonished at this! The same day I found the video, we received the letter. I asked Shawn how we got that letter. He explained that he was a partner of that ministry before we got married, and he had just changed the mailing address. Right at that moment we confessed to each other how God was speaking to both of us individually. Without any hesitation, we decided to go visit this pastor's church (James 4:8).

We went to spy out the land four times before we moved to Ohio to attend bible college.

R eview–Holding onto my human controlling power, my own way of thinking was blinding me from seeing the way out or the escape to deliverance. Freedom is a gift I can receive once I recognize that I need it and that I was wrong.

E ncouragement–Educate yourself on the matter of marriage and family, how it works, not according to society, but according to God's principles. Submit to God, to the authority of the Scriptures, and to those that God has put over you–in this case for me, to my husband because he is my head as the Bible says.

A pply–James 4:10; Philippians 2:3; Ephesians 5:21, 24; James 4:7; 2 Peter 1:5–8, 3:18; Colossians 1:9–10; Galatians 5:22–23; 2 Timothy 3:16–17; Hebrews 5:12–14; 1 Peter 2:1–25; Psalm 1:1–3; Matthew 7:24–27; 1 Corinthians 13:4–8.

L earn–I learned to put others before myself and not to think highly about myself, but to honor and respect others. Let go of the past and forgive. If I want God to use me, then I have to die in my own desires.

Chapter 3

My Most Exciting Experience!

When we arrived at this church in Columbus, Ohio, we wanted to kiss the ground–literally. That's how excited we were. We had amazing experiences on this trip. We met people from different parts of the world who were ready, as we were, to say "yes" to their calling. We didn't care about the sacrifice or the circumstances this decision would bring. Honestly, we didn't even know exactly what we were called to. We just knew that both of our hearts were being pulled (out of the boat) to do something great for the kingdom of God and that it would require us to trust God. This meant we would walk step by step in faith (Proverbs 3:5; 2 Corinthians 5:7).

Similar to the time Peter saw Jesus walking on water, he recognized his Master and asked, "Lord, tell me to come to you on the water." Jesus said, "Come," and he did. But at one point Peter looked down and started to drown. Fear of seeing the water too deep caused doubt to creep in. I can understand this because at one point we did the same (Matthew 14:24–31).

I remember one specific man we met on this trip. He told us his story, which encouraged us even more. He wanted to go to the

"Partners Weekend" very badly, but he had no money. One day, early in the morning in prayer, God told him to pack and go to the bus station. When he got there, a strange man was waiting for him and said, "Brother, I got your ticket" and they traveled together to the partner weekend (Matthew 21:22).

We witnessed people getting healed and saved. Christians were helping each other with the expenses of their trips. No one cared how long the services went, or how early they started. We woke up praying and reading the Word and went to sleep doing the same. This is the fire in our bones–the Word of God. We wanted more and God poured out His Spirit upon us. We started to have dreams and visions of our future in ministry. We might not have known the whole picture or the process, but just focusing on the future was enough for us to keep following that calling. We were like the fishermen who responded and obeyed quickly without hesitation when they heard Jesus passing by saying (with power and authority), "Follow me." Immediately, they left everything and followed Him. As promised by Christ, they went through a lot of persecution, hardship, tribulations, and death. It's a hard path to follow, that I know, but it's worth it (Matthew 4:18–22)!

We returned home after that trip, excited to see God's will be done here on Earth as it is in Heaven. Wherever I went I was talking to strangers about the love of Christ and His salvation (John 3:16). I was so excited about what God was going to do in our lives. I couldn't hide my emotions and my pride. Yes, I was very prideful about the whole thing. The idea that God was choosing us, and me specifically, made me feel as if I was "someone special" in the eyes of God. In my conversations with people in the church, I remember saying that God was sending me to the nations to preach the gospel. It's obvious that God is not looking for perfect people to use, He is looking for obedient vessels who are willing to leave everything and follow Him. One thing I know is that He'll change us along the way, if we allow Him (Isaiah 2:12).

We visited this pastor's church two more times. After coming back home from our third visit, we were convinced that we were supposed to move there and attend bible college. We were serious about this move and went back a fourth time to look for a place to live. We passed by an apartment complex and knew that this was the place for us to move. We stopped by and went inside the rental office (John 15:14).

There was a beautiful young lady who acted as if she was waiting for us, just like the man who was waiting for our friend at the bus station at the beginning of this chapter. It amazes me that before we make a move of faith in our lives, God goes ahead of us and sends His provision. We just have to believe and act in obedience. Like the Israelites at the Red Sea, no matter the persecution in front or behind them, when they were obedient to put their feet in the water, God opened it for them to cross through on dry land (Exodus 14:21–23).

This young lady at the rental office made us feel as if she were saying, "I have been waiting for you guys. What took you so long to get here?" We explained to her our plans, "We are leaving our jobs in New Jersey to move here with our two children and look for jobs so we can attend the bible college." In other words, we do not have jobs in Ohio, nor any prospective jobs lined up.

She completely ignored our employment situation and said, "Let me show you your apartment." She grabbed a key and started to walk, so we followed her (Proverbs 3:5–6).

Inside the beautiful two-bedroom apartment, she opened an empty room door and I asked, "Is this the laundry room?" "Yes!" she responded. I said, "Wait, but there's no laundry machines." She looked at me, closing the doors, and said, "I'll give you the machines for free."

She continued showing us the apartment and Shawn asked, "How much will we have to pay for the security deposit?" "If you have $100 right now, this apartment is yours," she said.

We were overwhelmed by this amazing deal. We thought that it was crazy! Just $600 a month for a two-bedroom luxury apartment, laundry machines for free, and only a $100 security deposit ... What??

I know what you're thinking right now. You probably want to pack and move to Ohio, but let me tell you what I tell everybody who says that when they hear this story. It wasn't natural, even though Ohio may be more affordable than New Jersey or other states, our situation was supernatural (Isaiah 65:24; Exodus 6:6-8). You will come to realize that as you continue reading.

We signed the contract and continued enjoying the remainder of the weekend. We did not miss one service. Our great experiences continued not only inside the church building, but at the stores, in restaurants, and other places where strange people prophesied over us, or I should say, confirmed to us what God already spoke to our hearts about our future (Jeremiah 29:11).

We came back to New Jersey with our new apartment contract in our hands. We had one month to prepare and pack for our move. Meanwhile, I felt in my heart the need to plant seeds because I believed that we would need an abundant harvest to walk the walk we were about to start (1 Corinthians 3:7; 9:10).

One day, I was praying and heard the Lord's inner voice say to me, "Tomorrow in church, there will be a lady worshiping next to you." He showed me everything she would be wearing. God continued to say, "I want you to put the bracelet on her wrist and tell her that she is a jewel for me."

My husband bought me a beautiful bracelet for Christmas the year prior. Yes, that's the one the Lord was talking about. Honestly, I wasn't concerned about what my husband would say if I gave it away. Shawn and I were both sold out for God and both were hearing from Him. This gave me the confidence to do this. It reminded me of the story when Jesus converted the water into wine. His mother, Mary, said to the servants, "Do whatever He tells you" (John 2:5).

I went to church the next day with the kids because Shawn had to work. There she was, the lady that God spoke to me about, worshiping next to me and wearing the exact same clothes He showed me. I put the bracelet on her wrist and told her what God told me to tell her. She started to cry and we both continued worshiping. After service, she told me how much that ministered to her heart and what she was going through at that moment (Psalm 139).

Shawn came home and I wanted to tell him about the bracelet. I started by saying, "Remember that bracelet you gave me?" To my surprise, he already knew it. He even knew the person I gave it to. Amazed at that, I asked him how he knew. He said, "On my way here God told me." (Jeremiah 33:3).

Then it happened again. God told me to write a check and bring it to church. He showed me the lady I was to bless. That Sunday at church, everything that God showed me and asked for happened. I wasn't going to miss anything. I wanted to follow every instruction that God was giving us to follow. It may not have made sense at the moment, but it did later (Proverbs 16:20).

We learned through the Word the principle of sowing and reaping, not just financially, but in time, love, honor, respect, faithfulness, etc. God gave us instructions and we followed them regardless of the circumstances or sometimes the sacrifice. We got so used to walking on this principle that it became our lifestyle. I don't mean that we give with one hand and wait to receive with the other, of course not. We give to please God and because it feels much better to give than to receive–to be a blessing than to get a blessing (Galatians 6:6–10)! We blessed a lot of people with everything we had, left our loved ones, and moved to what was, for us at that time, our promised land (Genesis 26:2–5).

One person I was excited to leave behind was someone close to my family. We just couldn't get along. For some reason it was very difficult for me to see this person or even hear their name being mentioned. No one knew this, but God. Nothing is hidden from Him (Hebrews 4:13).

On our way there, Shawn was driving a large U-Haul truck (It was his first time driving a truck that big) and I was driving my car (I couldn't even drive to the store by myself with confidence at this time). We were afraid, but we knew that God was going before us and that everything was going to be alright, no matter what (Deuteronomy 31:8).

I wish I could say that we had a smooth trip and that everything turned out fine because God was with us, but no, that's not how things work. He didn't promise a life without tribulations and circumstances. He promised that He would never leave us nor forsake us (Deuteronomy 31:6).

We always have to keep in mind that we live in a cursed world and things will just happen. Right before we crossed the New Jersey turnpike to enter into Pennsylvania at 5:00 a.m., the U-Haul truck had a flat tire. We needed roadside assistance to come and help. Later on, we stopped to eat at a rest stop and right when we were leaving that parking area, Shawn hit a pick-up truck on the side. As I was driving behind him, I could hear the noise and see the owner of the truck sitting on the back bed of his truck with his son enjoying their meal. Immediately, I began to speak in tongues, calling on the Holy Spirit for help. We both got out of our cars and were amazed by the whole thing. The owner of the truck looked at his car and said to us, "Don't worry. It's nothing, just go." What? I couldn't believe it. We both heard the noise of that U-Haul scratching that man's truck, but OK, thank you, Jesus. We continued on our way (Ephesians 1:11).

I was praying while driving, as my children were sleeping. When I looked up to the truck Shawn was driving in front of me, I saw these gigantic two angels, one on each side, and I felt this peace that came upon my heart. I started to thank God. At that point, I was more confident that we were safe. We finally arrived in Columbus, Ohio. We were excited, but extremely physically exhausted (Psalm 91:11).

Shawn stayed with the kids while I went to the rental office to get the key to our new apartment. There were completely different ladies working there than the lady we signed a contract with a month ago. The office atmosphere was not charming. This woman did not look friendly and was clearly not excited to see me (Proverbs 3:5).

I ignored her unwelcoming personality and said, "Hello" with a big smile on my face expecting she would smile back (and take out the balloons to celebrate with me!). To my surprise, she wasn't even expecting or waiting for us. She was there to do business, so I started by saying, "I'm here to pick up the key to our apartment" (still excited) (Psalm 28:7).

"What apartment?" She asked.

I told her the apartment address (still smiling).

"Nope," she said. "We did not contract that apartment to anybody. Maybe you came to the wrong apartment complex?" She began to tell me about some other apartments nearby.

For a moment I thought she might be right. She was not the lady we signed the contract with anyway. But then I thought, I can't be wrong. This is the address and the name of the apartment complex. What's going on?

She insisted that I should go to the apartment complex next to them, that maybe that was the one. Then a lady in another room came out and got involved in the situation, but she wasn't the lady we signed the contract with either. I began to describe the lady to them who originally helped us a month ago. Their answers confused me even more. "There's no lady with that name and description that works here. We are the two ladies that have been working here for years, no one else. I'm sorry," they said (Mark 5:36).

Very confused and disappointed, I went back to the car to get the kids and Shawn and the copy of our contract. We brought it to them and again Shawn explained the same story about the nice lady that we signed the contract with. The lady sitting in the front desk grabbed the contract copy from Shawn and opened a drawer that had many folders in it. She pulled out the original copy of our contract and said, "Guys, we don't know who that lady was, but you're right, here is your contract." Finally, she gave us the key (Isaiah 43:16–19). We couldn't believe it. What just happened? Who was that lady? Even today, I still think it was an angel sent by God. He is a God of the impossible (Luke 1:37)!

It was now time to unload the truck. We had brought our beautiful white couches with us. Back in New Jersey, Shawn kept telling me many times that they wouldn't fit through the apartment door, but I insisted. I asked God for permission to bring them and that He would make them smaller or the door wider. I prayed for this and was confident that I got God's approval. We carried the first couch together and there was just enough room for the couches to go through. I tried not to look at Shawn in his eyes, but we both started to laugh. I rejoiced with this, not because I was right, but because once again, I heard from God and my faith was working (Hebrews 11:1).

We finally were all situated and the time for registration at the bible college came. We registered but couldn't start classes yet because we didn't have the tuition money. I remember that day, we both walked out of the line very disappointed–without words. It was complete silence between us. There were a lot of students sent by their pastors or family members who paid their tuition in full. Unfortunately, we didn't have that. The church we were attending in New Jersey was affiliated with a different type of ministry than the one that we were sent by God to go to. Yes, you read correctly, God sent us, and that's why I was confident that He would provide. It was not the church's responsibility to do God's work. He sent us, not them. For men will not get glory, but God (Romans 4:20)!

At the time, I thought that God wasn't providing, and I started to feel nervous. My perfect and prideful plan was failing. Remember that back in New Jersey I was telling people that God was sending us here and that we were going to go to the nations to preach the gospel. Yet, here we were told to leave the registration line, giving more room for those who had the money to proceed with their registration (Isaiah 55:8).

Two weeks went by and there was no money for our tuition, or for anything else. This is where our faith began to shake. We started to think that we were wrong for moving to Ohio, that God did not call us to leave our jobs and family, that our dream was a false hope. Maybe we were better in New Jersey? Maybe we didn't hear God? As most married couples would do at this moment, we started to blame one another. Shawn desperately tried to find a job but couldn't get an interview. For the first time in our marriage, there was no food for our children. Starting bible college was out of reach and impossible. The conflict in our marriage was back. I felt angry with Shawn and God. The question came—just like the snake asked Eve in the garden to confuse her at the moment of temptation—Did God really say (Genesis 3:1)?

After Shawn applied to different manufacturing companies without success, he was so excited that he heard from God to apply in a certain place. He took me for a ride to show me the place—a carwash! Yes, after working as a supervisor in big companies, making good money, now he was going to wash cars. He also found a part-time job in a glue factory. The owner of the carwash called him immediately and asked questions like, "Why do you want to work here?" According to his resume he was overqualified but, thank God, he got the job and very quickly became co-manager of the carwash. This carwash represented our little cloud for the rain that was to come later (1 Kings 18:44).

Even with Shawn working two part time jobs, it wasn't enough to sustain our family. We were very tight financially. What is so funny is that I wasn't looking for a job. Since I married, I was a stay-at-home mom. That worked for us back in New Jersey when Shawn had a good job, but now? I had the mentality that "the man has to provide." I believe that was just an excuse for my laziness. It was different when the kids were little, but when they were all in school, I stayed home, even though I was a healthy woman with all kinds of financial issues. How much could I clean, cook, or do laundry? Honestly, with the kind of mind I had and the issues in my heart, this was a big mistake. Staying at home affected me tremendously because I had more time to allow my mind to go crazy with negative thoughts. As a preacher once said, "Stinking thinking!" I totally agree that man is the provider of his home, but God created us (wives) to be their helpers. Shouldn't we obey God and take this to heart and do our job, especially in hard times (Genesis 2:18)?

It was 9 p.m. one night and Shawn wasn't back yet from his second temporary job. I was concerned that there was no food left to feed our two children, so I went to pray. I was bending down on my knees to ask God for provision, when a noise at my door interrupted me. I looked through the little hole but there was nobody, but I knew I heard something. Even my oldest daughter heard it. She came running from her room and asked me, "Who's knocking?" She went to look through the window and said, "Mommy, there's no one at the door, but there's a lot of bags."

I was nervous to open the door because I didn't know anybody. I wasn't sure if it was a good idea to open that door, but when I saw that my daughter was right, that there were a lot of bags, then I opened the door. I was amazed by what I saw–bags and bags full of groceries! I couldn't believe it! It was as if I went grocery shopping myself. The food items were exactly what we like to eat. God provided even before I asked Him. This happened many times. He wasn't going to let our children starve (Matthew 6:33).

These experiences kept my head above water and prevented me from drowning in fear. Also, there was a voice that I heard constantly. It was the voice of our pastor back in New Jersey. His messages about faith encouraged me to keep trusting, keep believing, don't lose hope (1 Peter 5:10).

Honestly, not having the money for the bible college tuition was devastating to us because that was the main reason we moved there. I thought that God forgot us. It didn't matter how much I heard or saw God making a way where there was no way in our lives. As hard times came, it was easy for doubt and unbelief to come in and take over. It was difficult for me to understand that God is a promise keeper (2 Corinthians 1:20).

I remember a lady that I met at church. She came to visit one night and brought me to her car. She began to tell me her opinion about my husband. She said, "Let me tell you, you are all suffering because of the kind of husband that you have. He is a lazy bum. He needs to go find a real job and work hard and forget the idea of bible college, blah, blah, blah."

I was listening to my "sister-in-Christ" and was blindly receiving everything into my mind from someone who didn't know my husband. When she was done with her "encouragement", I went inside my house and found my husband asleep. What do you think happened? I woke Shawn up. "Wake up, lazy bum! We are suffering because of you. You need to work a real job."

Yes, I repeated like a machine, word for word, to my husband what that sister-in-Christ told me. I fought that night with all the passion and anger I had at the time. Shawn just cried, surprised at my words and my reaction until I felt so horrible and guilty because I knew I was wrong. I allowed a strange person to put ungodly thoughts towards my husband in my mind and the most disgraceful words in my mouth. What happened? I thought I was changed and transformed? But there were still things in my heart that I never dealt with and they were coming up little by little. It doesn't matter how spiritual I thought I was, or how much faith I had, whatever was in my heart was coming out with my uncontrolled emotions. Instead of dealing with it, I ignored it. I knew my husband was applying to many companies, and he was at the same time following God's instruction and calling for our lives. I even agreed with his decision to attend bible college and move to Ohio, but my emotions were stirred up and it was difficult to control them. Knowing the truth that could make me free was not enough. I needed to apply it to my own heart and recognize that I needed it, that I was wrong and that I wanted to change. I needed to humble myself before God, but up to this point I had not done that (James 4:10).

I started to cry and confess to Shawn about our surprise visit that night. I felt horrible and once again was used by the devil to destroy my own marriage. But who thought that a sister-in-Christ from our new amazing church would come like a devil dressed as a sheep with an assignment? Shawn forgave me and we decided to stay far away from her in the future.

I chose to write about this experience here because we need to open our eyes. We can't allow just anybody to come into our lives and give us advice. I don't care who they are or what title or position they have. Wisdom protects us (Proverbs 4:6–7).

Another time, as I was praying for my marriage, God ministered to my heart with a specific story. He said, "Remember when Jesus walked into Jerusalem and the people were screaming, 'Hosanna, Hosanna' The Pharisees told him to tell the people to be quiet. Jesus responded, 'If they are quiet, the rocks will shout out'?"

"Yes Lord," I responded, thinking about the story. He continued, "The same in your marriage, if you don't worship your husband, the rocks will." I was amazed by His teaching. Of course, He did not mean for me to bow down and worship my husband. He meant that I needed to care for, honor, and respect him (Luke 19:37–40).

Chapter 3 My Most Exciting Experience!

God is perfect in all of His ways. His grace is sufficient (2 Corinthians 12:9). One day our church had a picnic and while everyone was enjoying it, I went to the back of the church to pray. "God, you brought us here. You sent us to this bible college, where is the money? God answer me please. How are we going to do this?" I cried out of desperation. Suddenly, I heard a car coming very fast. It stopped right in front of me. An elderly woman came out and asked me, "Excuse me, why are you crying?" "I'm not crying, I'm praying," I responded. She continued, "What are you praying for?" I told her our story, how God sent us here to bible college, but we had no money for the tuition. She bent over and took some music CDs out of her bag and said, "I'm a singer for the Lord and I came here all the way from West Virginia, looking for the man of God (she meant the pastor of that mega-church). Here." she said, handing me her CDs. It was strange, but right there, she realized that she was wearing the same clothes that she had on for one of her CD covers. She was laughing about it and asked me for my name and phone number. She said, "I'm going back home right now." She quickly left in her car and sped out of the parking lot (Psalm 18:30).

I thought this was very weird. I remembered looking at her feet. I saw something very special. It was as if she was sent by God just for me. My husband came and asked who that lady was. I explained what happened. We went home and played her CDs, and the presence of the Lord filled our room through her voice. Three days later, she called me and said, "That day, after I heard your story, I got what I needed. Faith came back to me, and today I want you to have what you need. I paid your tuition to the bible college."

I couldn't believe it. I was overwhelmed with happiness. I was thanking God for it. I told my husband, but for some reason I said it in a very prideful way. "My tuition is paid. Pray, and pray very hard, so you can get yours paid, too" (Isaiah 2:12).

God has never finished teaching me the way I should go. He knows the depths of my heart and He wants me to be free. He allows things in my path for a reason, for my own good. He sees my heart and He knows what's hiding. He wants us to be completely free. He, as our Father, knows what is best for each of us. We have to know His Word to know His will and instruction for our individual lives. He is a good God. A good Father (1 Samuel 16:7).

The same night after the lady called me to say that she paid my tuition, I was awakened by the feeling of someone shaking my leg. I opened my eyes and heard, "Come to my presence. I need to give you instructions." I knew who that was. I did not need to think twice. I immediately went into His presence in my living room and the first thing He said was, "Why do you go around telling everyone that I gave you that husband and you treat him like this?" It was as if a video recording machine of memories came to my mind—every time I disrespected my husband. That really hurt me. I knew that I was wrong, but I didn't care so much. I always thought it was Shawn's fault because he made me treat him like that. But at that moment, I saw the truth, my eyes were being opened (Ephesians 1:18). I was hurt and I was hurting my husband. It was time to end this. God said to me, "He (Shawn) is the head of this household. I (God) created him with his abilities to manage his home. Who are you to not trust his abilities? He goes first. Before you go to the nations, you go home and be a wife and a mother. I put that tuition money in your hands as a seed for your marriage. Choose today, death or life in your marriage, choose life" (Deuteronomy 30:15–20).

I won't lie and say to you that it was easy for me. It was not. Even though I knew exactly what God was asking me to do, I was afraid. Afraid of letting go of my controlling ways of living and my rollercoaster-up-and-down emotional decision making. Letting go of my power was painful, but I needed to choose and this time I chose life!

I cried in repentance the whole night, asking God for forgiveness. Later that morning, I asked my husband to forgive me for taking the place that belonged to him in our home and for being so disrespectful. I also told him to get ready and go start attending the bible college. Yes, I gave up bible college and gave my husband my tuition money because I needed to obey God and go to a different place to learn–home. I needed to learn to be a Christian wife (a wife of noble character) and to be a mother (Proverbs 12:4; 31:10–31). Let me tell you, since the day of my obedience to choose life, my marriage turned around in an amazing way, all because this is how God intended marriage to be when He says, "Wives, submit to your husbands" (Ephesians 5:22).

I learned that I am created to be a rib to help and support, not to be the head. Things started to get in the right place as God intended in my home. My husband finally became the head of the household. I allowed him to make decisions. I learned to support him, even when I think he is making a bad decision. I, by the wisdom of God, give him my opinion. Then I go to Jesus in prayer and tell Him to take control of the situation. I learned to be at peace and confident that everything would be all right because of my submission to God to honor and respect my husband. This allowed God to take control. My obedience unlocked my blessings (James 4:7).

I continued reading my bible. Proverbs 31:10–31 changed my life. It was like a mirror that showed me who I really was and how much I needed to let go and let God. I desired to be the type of wife the Bible talks about. She is very kind and gentle. She is strong and also a hard worker, which made me more careful not to confuse faith with a magic wand or think that I could just snap my fingers in Jesus' name and "boom" it happens. That's not how this works. We have to give Him something to multiply. The wife the Bible talks about gave the Lord a lot to work with. She not only was blessed, but she was a blessing to her husband and her family, and I wanted to be like her. It was time to grow up (Ephesians 4:15–19)!

I realized there would not be a miracle if the disciples didn't bring Jesus the five loaves of bread and two fish to feed the five thousand (Luke 9:10–17). There would be no wine if the servants did not bring the water (John 2:1–11). When Peter was distressed and Jesus asked, "What troubles you, Peter?" "The tax collector asked for your taxes and mine," Peter answered. Jesus told Peter to go to the lake and throw out his line–in other words, "Go to work, Peter." He continued to instruct him. "Take the first fish you catch; open its mouth and you will find a four-drachma coin. Take it and give it to them for my tax and yours" (Matthew 17:24–27). We have to read and understand the Bible to understand how Jesus' miracles happened. He is powerful and Almighty. He can do anything, but He has given us instructions to follow so He can multiply and do miracles. God promises to establish the work of our hands, so we need to put our hands to work (Psalm 90:17).

Finally, I started to see the heavy load on my husband's shoulders. I took the step to help him by going to look for a job. I found one in a hotel, cleaning rooms. I also started to find ways to bless bible college students. I cooked meals for them, and I encouraged them to put their eyes on Jesus, the miracle worker (Mark 9:23).

Walking on water–believing that God will faithfully and constantly provide–is not an easy thing to do. Shawn has always been a man that lives on a budget. He told me that we were short on money to pay our bills. Without hesitation, we continued paying our tithes and praying, asking God to supply our needs. I was in a store buying groceries as my children began to play with a strange lady's kids. Because of that, we introduced ourselves and became friends. When I was leaving the store, she came to me and said, "The Lord just told me to bless you with this money." She gave me the exact amount we needed to pay our bills (Philippians 4:19; Proverbs 10:3).

Miracles were continuing. For over three years, we thought that Shawn couldn't have children and that was one of my biggest desires. I wanted two children with him. I even volunteered at the church's children's ministry as a seed, believing for two of my own (Psalm 127:3–5).

A month or two later, after I chose life in my marriage, I was doing my work (being a helper). I was at the hotel working my housekeeping job and saw a pear in one of the rooms I was cleaning that day. I wanted to eat it so badly, but I couldn't. It wasn't mine. Now I know how Eve felt when she had the temptation to eat the fruit. Immediately, I remembered that the hotel had orange juice downstairs, so I ran away from my temptation (that pear!) to ask my supervisor if I could have some orange juice. She said, "Yes". Oh, how I wish Eve did the same! I grabbed that glass of orange juice and drank it like water. Then I went to continue working, but something wasn't feeling right. I felt so sick that I went home early. I laid down and all of a sudden, I realized that there was a possibility of me being pregnant. I got up and ran to the store to buy a pregnancy test. Yes, I was pregnant. I couldn't believe it. Once again, God was showing me that He is a faithful promise keeper (Luke 1:45)!

Later, when Shawn came home, I told him. We were both very excited and couldn't believe what was happening. Shawn grabbed the pregnancy test and locked himself in the bathroom. When he came out, I asked what he was doing. He said, "I was reading all the instructions making sure we were right." We knew the responsibility that was upon our shoulders and in the natural world, it didn't make sense. We were struggling financially. Shawn was a bible college student and working part-time jobs. But God knows best. He knows the right time (2 Peter 3:8).

We didn't know yet if it was a boy or a girl. A friend of mine invited me to go eat at a Chinese restaurant. We stopped first by my husband's job, the carwash, to tell him where we were going. As we arrived, a lady from my church was talking to Shawn. She was so happy to see me because she came to prophesy over our baby. According to her words, we understood that the baby was a boy and that his name was Daniel. I was so excited about that. I love the story of Daniel.

My friend and I finally got to the restaurant and, while we were eating, a strange lady sitting right behind me turned around and asked me, "Ma'am, are you pregnant?" "Yes," I responded. She told me the exact prophecy as the other lady. At that point, I had no doubt that these prophecies were from God. My baby would be a boy and his name would be Daniel. We finished eating and my friend asked for the bill. The server answered, "You owe nothing. Your God took care of the bill. It's all paid." At that point, I was in shock of everything! My friend and I couldn't stop thanking God because we both witnessed something that day. I shared everything with Shawn, and we kept it in our hearts (Luke 2:19).

As the cold of that winter settled in, we were struggling to pay our heat bill. The gas company shut off our heat because we were unable to pay for many months. We didn't know what to do. We went to church that day and when we were leaving, I noticed that a lady at the product table next to the door had a small electric heater blowing by her feet. My family's need made me boldly go to her and ask her to please let us borrow that heater for one night. She was not happy to lend it to us but did agree to let us use it. We went home and gathered all the blankets we had in the house and slept all together in the same bed to warm ourselves with our shared body heat. The next day we returned the heater that we borrowed, but a lady called and said, "God told me to call you and ask you how I can help you." She paid our gas bill immediately. We had heat back in the house (Luke 12:24)!

One thing I know is this, some people like to tell the miracle, but me, I love to tell people the story before the miracle. God is amazing. We will go through trials and circumstances, but we must trust God no matter what (James 1:12).

Finally, I went to my next doctor's visit and to my surprise, he told me that my baby was a girl. What just happened? I was driving my car on my way home totally confused, "God, did I miss something?" I got home and went right to His presence. I had questions to ask

Him, and He responded, "Imagine the spirit of Daniel in a woman."
Right there, I knew that her name was Daniela.

We had nothing yet for this baby, but one day, someone knocked
on my door. It was a man from our church. "Come out," he said.
I came out and he opened the door of a van. He said, "This is
a blessing for your baby." A family from our church sent him to
bless us. He brought us everything a mother desires for her baby
girl: a crib, a diaper-changing table, bouncy toys, clothes, a car seat,
books, and a stroller. Everything (Philippians 4:19)!

Later, a group of friends from church did a baby shower for us and
we had even more. I had so much that there was not enough room
in our two-bedroom apartment to contain everything that God was
blessing us with because it was His time. Perfect timing (Luke 6:38,
Malachi 3:10)!

Soon after Daniela was born, we realized that now we needed
another car. I wasn't working anymore, and Shawn was driving
everyone around to school, doctor's appointments, food shopping,
then his two jobs and bible college. It was difficult for him. If we
had another car, I could be doing all of that instead, so we once
again put our faith to work. We prayed and asked God to bless us
with a car in Jesus' name. The day we requested our car to the Lord
was a Sunday. On Monday, Shawn heard that there was a married
couple at the bible college that needed money for their tuition.
Shawn felt in his heart to bless them with everything we had–the
$100 that we had in the bank. Shawn wrote the check. Remember,
just one year prior, we were in this couple's same situation.

He stopped by the house to eat really quickly before he went to
work and told me all about it. My answer was, "That better be
God". As a mother, I was concerned because we had no money
for food as he gave our last $100 away. What's so crazy is that the
same day, at the carwash, a coworker, who didn't know we were
believing for a car, prophesied to Shawn, "God is about to bless you

with a red car." He came home that night and told me about his coworker's prophecy. It felt as if we were getting very close to our miracle. The next day, early in the morning, I broke a piggy bank to look for coins and one-dollar bills to venture out to the store to get something for our children to eat. I was walking by the deli department and a worker looked at me and said, "Oh my gosh, honey!" She threw everything she had in her hands and started to walk towards me. I got a little bit nervous. She got close to me and asked, "Honey, do you need a car?" For a moment, I thought she said, "card," for me to pay for my groceries, but at the same time I thought she meant "car". I was a little bit confused and I think she realized it. So, she looked at my eyes and repeated it very clearly and mimicked her hands, "Do you need a car?" I felt like Ralphie, the little boy in the Christmas Story movie when Santa asked him what he wanted and he said, a "football" when he wanted a B.B. gun. Ralphie said to himself, inside his own mind, "Wake up, stupid!"

I looked at her and I said, "Yes." "The Lord just told me to bless you with a car," she said. "What church do you go to?" she asked. We found out we went to the same church, but because our church was very large, we had never seen each other before. "Are you going to church tomorrow?" She asked. "Yes," I said. "Meet me at the right side of the parking lot, I'll be there with your car." I thanked her and took off running. I paid for my groceries and went back home. On my way home, the devil started to play games in my mind, "Did she say, car or card? Oh no, she said card ... No, she mimicked her hands. She said, 'car.'" I yelled, "Stop it, devil! Stop! Even if she said card, I believe that she will be there tomorrow with my car!"

I got home and told Shawn everything. We rejoiced together, thanking God for our miracle. Wednesday came and we went to church. We got to the north side of the parking lot and there she was, with our "red" car–not just a car, but a "red" car. I introduced my husband to her, and she gave us the key and the title. God is awesome. Shawn brought the car to show to his coworker, as he prophesied this red car days earlier. We all were amazed by what God does for those who believe him (Ephesians 3:20–21; Matthew 21:22).

Daniela was three months old and because it took us three years to get pregnant, we never thought that it would only take three months to get pregnant again. I knew it the moment I conceived. I ran to buy a pregnancy test. As I waited for the results, I covered my eyes and, with tears, I begged God for that test to be negative. Slowly, I opened one eye and looked, "Oh my, no. God, no." Thinking that Daniela was too little for me to have another one and knowing our financial situation, I cried with disappointment. Again, I was seeing with my natural eyes and nothing made any sense to me. However, God's timing is perfect. He spoke to my heart right at that moment and said, "He will be little, but he will kill giants." Right there, I knew that he was a boy and that his name was David. I visited the doctor and he confirmed that it was a boy. I told him, "I know, and his name is David" (1 Samuel 17).

Once again, a group of friends threw us a baby shower. It got to a point that I had to ask people to please stop sending things. Later on, a family that we did not know well, continually blessed us until the time we moved back to New Jersey. We did not talk over the phone or have meals of fellowship together with this family. They were just obedient to God. We never once had to buy clothes or shoes for our son. He had everything he needed (John 14:23).

Our new normal began to set in. We had four kids to feed, rent to pay, school tuition, and all of the expenses to survive in this world. At this point, I couldn't go back to work because of our two babies, so everything was on Shawn's shoulders again, but wait until you see what I'm about to share with you in my next chapter (2 Samuel 22:33).

Miracles happen because He is Real!

R eview–My heart was not changed and transformed, but God wanted to use me the way I was. He does not call perfect people to use, He calls obedient vessels. If we follow His instructions, He will change our hearts because it is impossible to walk with God each day and not be transformed.

E ncouragement–Be obedient and submissive to God. Do whatever He asks you to do, even when it does not make sense. Be a doer of His Word. Walk by faith, not by sight. Be a hard worker. Pay your tithes. Choose life!

A pply–Proverbs 3:5–6; Matthew 17:20; Mark 16:17; Mark 9:23; John 11:40–42; Romans 8:28; Jeremiah 29:11; Galatians 2:20; Romans 3:23; Philippians 1:6; James 1:5; 2 Peter 3:9; Ephesians 4:26; Hosea 4:6; Romans 8:1–39.

L earn–I learned to trust God with all of my heart and not in my own understanding, but in all my ways I acknowledge Him, and He makes my path straight. My obedience unlocked my blessings.

Chapter 4

My Most Difficult Experience!

Everything was beautiful. I was a very busy mother, which was good because I could easily ignore the thoughts in my mind that were manifesting a spirit of fear. It doesn't matter who you are, in this world we will have tribulations (John 16:33).

During our first three years in Ohio, I received five different phone calls from my family back in New Jersey, letting me know that five family members passed away one after another. After the third phone call, I started to have frequent panic attacks. I noticed that any time my phone would ring, I would get anxious, especially if it was any of my family members calling me (Psalm 94:19).

Throughout my pregnancy with David, I had some unusual symptoms. Sometimes I would have difficulties swallowing. It wasn't that bad, and it only happened once in a while. Therefore, I didn't think much about it or feel that I should tell somebody. I just continued living life as normal. Many times, because of fear, we make the mistake of living in denial instead of facing our problems. I thought I could just believe in silence for a supernatural healing. I didn't want to even think that I needed to go visit a doctor or take any type of medication. I could never imagine God using doctors and medicine to heal people (Proverbs 2:6).

One Sunday at church, our Pastor gave an instruction to the leaders to pass around prayer cloths for those who needed a miracle. When that prayer cloth came to my hands, I paused. I wanted to think about what I should ask for. Immediately, my youngest brother came to my mind. He moved to Texas two years prior and never contacted us, which was very concerning to my family, especially to our mother (Acts 19:11–12).

My request was simple but not easy in my eyes, "God, please change my brother's life." I clearly heard in my spirit, "I'm not only going to change his life, but I'll turn his life around." I became so excited I put the prayer cloth, attached to my prayer request, back in the envelope and dropped it in the offering bucket.

After church, we went home and had lunch. At 2 p.m. that same afternoon, I had a phone call. Are you ready for this?

It was my brother!

I couldn't believe it. Remember, I didn't hear from him for two long years since he had relocated to Texas. Yet, the day I put my request in, he called me. Coincidence? I strongly believe not. I believe in His sovereignty. God orchestrated everything (Deuteronomy 10:21).

"Hello!" I said.

"Hey, it's me. I'm in Cincinnati. Give me your address. I'm coming to visit you right now."

Oh my gosh. I went crazy. I was still on the phone and I motioned to Shawn, telling him that my brother was on the phone. That's how excited I was. I hung up the phone and I couldn't believe it. God you are amazing! This reminded me of when Peter was in jail and God delivered him in a miraculous way. He brought him to the house of the people who were asking God in prayer to release him, but they couldn't believe it when their answer was right in front of them. "Who's at the door?" they asked. "It's Peter" was the reply. "Stop, Peter is in jail," they said. It was the same with me. For my brother to show up all the way from Texas to Ohio the same day I asked God to change his life was something that, to the human mind, was impossible (Acts 12:3–19).

I was super excited. I told my husband and my children. We were all completely amazed. I thought I needed to preach the whole Bible to my brother. I ran to my room to pray and I heard God saying to me, "Just love him." For a moment I thought, yes, I will love him by telling him the Word, but that's not what He meant. I knew exactly what He wanted me to do and I was ready and prepared to do it–to spend time with and listen to what my brother had to say. I was to serve him (1 Corinthians 16:14).

Finally, my brother arrived with his girlfriend. They had a two-year-old son at that time, but he was back home in Texas with her family. They shared with me the exciting news that there was another baby on the way (Jeremiah 1:5).

The first thing I did was call my mom and surprise her with my brother's voice. She was so happy and amazed at the whole thing. Understandably, she took a moment to admonish him for not contacting us. He laughed like it was a funny joke and promised to find a way to call her once in a while.

As we ate, I stood at the table talking to him and his girlfriend for a couple of hours. I sat next to him and stretched my arm around him to give some long overdue sisterly affection. He was wearing a long heavy necklace that held a cross. That started the conversation about Jesus our Savior. My brother opened his heart like never before. He confessed to me that he received Jesus as his Lord and Savior years before with our own father. He said that he needed to serve Him and shared with me the desire that he had to look for a church to attend with his family. I encouraged him to do it as soon as he returned back home (Romans 10:9–10).

My brother always had a big smile and sparkling eyes. It was natural for him to always joke around, but this time I noticed that he was very serious about things and his eyes looked weak, as if he was deep in thought. I can say now that his heart was discerning the future. He looked in my eyes and asked me about each member of our family. He started with our brothers and sisters and ended with our parents. What amazed me later was that for each name he mentioned he made a comment from the depths of his heart about that specific person. He talked about many things that happened in our childhood and how he had forgiven and understood some people who opened wounds and inflicted much pain in his heart. He talked about his life and family relationships as they became clearer to him.

Finally, we decided to go have fun in the pool at the apartment complex. Once again, while everybody swam, he continued his confession, but this time it was about his girlfriend and his own children—the loves of his life. He had already picked the name of his baby who was in the womb. He wanted to make sure that I knew it, even when no one in his family or hers had that name. He chose it because he wanted the child to have a biblical name. This would become very significant in a different situation years later (Mark 11:25; Proverbs 16:9).

He jumped into the pool and swam underwater back and forth two or three times. I remember thinking he swims like a fish. He came out and we went back home. That's when he told me that they were leaving early in the morning. I was so disappointed. Yes, they came just for one night. His company sent him to deliver a truckload of materials from Texas to Ohio. Before I put my prayer request in the offering bucket, God already answered it by sending him on his way to my house (1 John 5:14–15).

He sat in the living room watching TV with my oldest son. Once again, his eyes were intensely staring. I thought that he might be tired, so I told him to go to sleep, but he refused. He wanted to stay there sitting next to me. Even if we weren't talking anymore, he wanted to be by my side a little bit longer. While he watched the TV, I tried to look at him, trying to discern what was wrong. Why was I seeing a sad look on his face? I tried to convince myself that it was because he was tired, even though my heart was telling me something that I didn't want to accept.

Finally, he went to sleep. The next morning, he woke up early, ate breakfast, and I asked, "Can I pray for you?" He said, "Yes." I prayed for him and once again I felt this heavy grief in my heart. I couldn't understand or describe my feeling, but I knew that it was something that was bringing sadness to me. All I wanted to do was to stop my brother from leaving. I wanted to cry and tell him, "Please don't go," but I couldn't. How could I explain to him or his girlfriend my feelings? I just kept rebuking the thoughts of death and the sense of bad feelings that increasingly became some kind of grief (Hebrews 5:14).

As I walked him out to his car, the moment came. We had to say goodbye. He kissed my forehead and said, "I love you" and left. For some reason that kiss reverberated deep in my soul. I stood outside looking at his truck, waving to him until I could not see his car anymore. I still remember his eyes in the rear-view mirror, looking at me all the way down my short block. I walked back into my apartment and couldn't stop crying. Shawn tried to comfort me by telling me that I would see him again. I remember telling him that I didn't understand why I was feeling the way I was feeling. Something was not right. I could not explain the mysterious feeling of sorrow that was deep in my heart (1 Corinthians 3:16).

Thankfully, they got to Texas fine. They called me to thank me for everything. My brother's girlfriend shared with me how excited he was to go to church. I continued encouraging them to find a local church home and to serve God with all of their lives (Deuteronomy 11:13).

Two weeks later, just days before I was about to give birth to my baby boy, my mom came to visit to help me, as I had to balance taking care of a newborn with three other children in the home. I was sitting on my couch when I saw my mom walking from the bedroom into the kitchen to prepare one of her delicious meals. She happened to be wearing black and white clothes, which for some reason got my attention. I trembled in fear and felt as if I knew that death was taking place somewhere. I can't explain how I was fighting these thoughts and trying to rebuke them, but my heart was so alarmed or conscious of something. Please do not take this wrong. I'm not a superstitious person. I don't feel this way when I see someone wearing black and white. I believe that this was God preparing my heart and I kept resisting it. Remember, I was nine months pregnant when all of this was happening. I tried to control myself by distracting my mind with the TV. Then my mom's phone rang. Within seconds, she was uncontrollably crying, "No, no, I'm going to die. No, please no!" (Hebrews 4:13).

I got up and saw my mom emotionally broken. This was the moment I put everything together. I knew exactly what happened. But I asked, "What happened, Mom? Mom, please tell me what happened." "Call Shawn," she said, looking at me with her eyes, covering the pain to prevent harming her pregnant daughter. She continued telling me, "I can't tell you, call Shawn." I grabbed her arm and I said, "Mom, I know. My brother, he died. My brother is dead, Mom, I know, he is dead!" She looked at me in shock and asked, "How do you know?" My mind, heart, and my spirit were connected and graced with supernatural strength. My heart was prepared for this painful moment. I sat my mom down and told her everything from the prayer cloth, to the moment of her phone call. This story gave my mom so much peace, strength, and courage from above. God's grace is sufficient (2 Corinthians 12:9; Isaiah 43:2)!

Later that afternoon, Shawn went to get the mail and said to me, "There was no mail, just one thing." He gave it to me. It was the prayer cloth with a letter from our Pastor saying that he is in agreement with my request (Psalm 139:16; Jeremiah 33:3).

Allow me to ask you one question, Who makes these things up? Who? God is real!

My brother's body was buried in Honduras. Tragically, I couldn't go with my family because I was giving birth to my baby boy, David, at the same time. But God knew it all. I was the only one who had the privilege to see, talk, and hug my brother two weeks before he died. These amazing memories that we built in such a short time are forever in my heart (Matthew 10:28).

In prayer, I asked God about this whole situation. He said to me, you have a choice, will you glorify Satan's name or mine? Right there, I realized that Satan took my brother's life, but God saved his soul and orchestrated everything for our family's own good. I might not have answers to my "whys", but one thing I know is that God knows every heart better than I do. Years later, I found out the reason for the car accident and it all made sense. God knew that my brother would be at the wrong time and in the wrong place. We have free will and God will never stop us from making our own choices. I'm sorry, but it is the truth that sets us free (John 8:32)!

I was crying one day, looking through my window thinking of how much I would love to meet my nephews, my brother's two sons. I heard on the inside, "When the time is right, I will bring you to meet them." I thanked God for this. I believed Him and I kept that in my heart as a promise that one day would come to pass, and it did (Isaiah 41:13).

After all of this, the weird symptoms began to increase in my body. I started to search my heart as I heard some preachers teach that sometimes bitterness and unforgiveness are the reasons for sickness attacking our bodies. To my surprise, the first thing that came to my mind was that person close to my family who I couldn't get along with. One day, Shawn mentioned their name and I lost it. "I hate her!" I screamed. Shawn looked at me and said, "My love, did you hear your words? You are not talking like a Christian." Right at that moment, I felt a knot in my heart. I knew that I was holding bitterness against this person. The Bible tells us that it is not what enters the mouth that defiles a man, it's what comes out of the mouth that defiles a man because it comes from the heart (Matthew 15:11).

I cried out to God because I had no idea how to let go of my anger towards this person. How could I undo the knot? I knew it was there. I just needed to think about it and check my own heart. I could sense the anger, bitterness, and unforgiveness. I started to cry in repentance, asking God to forgive me and to help me, because somehow, I did this to myself (Ephesians 4:31–32; Matthew 18:21–22).

I felt Jesus come into the room. I could feel His presence as He began to minister to my heart by telling me things that only He could know, "Hurting people hurt people. Everyone gives what is in their hearts." This opened my eyes. I realized that this person had nothing against me. It was nothing personal. God continued saying, "As I sent Moses to deliver my people from bondage, I sent you to this person's life to bring deliverance through my love in you, but you allow 'Pharaoh' to control you and manipulate you with harmful words and actions" (Exodus 14:13).

Right at that moment I was free. I repented and let it go by allowing the love of God to work in my heart and to exchange hate for Christ's love. This person is still the same, there has been no change yet, but what changed is my heart. I learned that we need to see others with the eyes of God, not with our own natural eyes. Thank you, Jesus (Psalm 51:10–19)!

My heart was delivered from this bitterness, but unfortunately my physical body was still being attacked by unusual symptoms. I couldn't swallow and I was losing a lot of weight, but I was more captivated by the miracles that were happening all around me than what my own body was experiencing. I ignored the issues because I was afraid to accept the reality that my body was fighting an unknown sickness. I ignored the symptoms, hoping that they would go away and disappear by themselves. I focused more on other needs where I could use my faith more easily, like our financial needs, for example. That was something personal, but not too personal, in the sense that it was a need that didn't hurt my physical body. I didn't really feel it and it was easy to trust God in that area of my life. It happened automatically, probably because I was getting used to seeing God providing in an amazing way since we said, "Yes," to His call in our life (Matthew 6:21).

At this time, we were short on our rent money. I very easily trusted that God was going to take care of it. That same day, we received a check in the mail with the exact amount we needed and a note from our friends from out of state, saying that this money was specifically for our rent. We experienced this many times as I had no doubt that God is my provider (Philippians 4:19).

Another miracle we saw at this time was the promotion Shawn received. He was still working at the car wash. Remember, in my last chapter, I mentioned that this car wash was the little cloud for us because of the large storm of blessing that this brought later on. It was made possible because of Shawn's obedience to do what God asked him to do, regardless of the circumstances or how it looks in the natural eyes. An important thing I want to mention here is that we never stopped tithing. This is critical and extremely important. If we had situations where we had to choose between tithing or paying our bills, we always chose tithing. We couldn't steal from God to pay our bills. Our tithes belong to God, always have been and always will be (Leviticus 27:30).

I remember we thought that one particular day was going to be like any other day–just like the Samaritan woman. She was doing the usual, but God had another plan to meet her at her everyday spot– the well. Sometimes just when we least expect things, they happen. Our pastor's executive assistant came to the car wash to take care of his car and he met Shawn. What a divine connection! Who would think that God would use this car wash as a step for something greater in our lives? Later on, this man was looking to hire someone to take the position of Family Life Ministries at the church. He felt in his heart that the man at the car wash "washing cars" was the man he was praying for. And yes, he offered the job and Shawn gladly accepted it. Never overlook or despise your small beginnings (Zechariah 4:10).

Some people even with great financial needs in their lives won't take minimum wage jobs because they want to jump to higher paying jobs right away. That's not how this works. We start from the bottom and God makes our way up to the top. We need to humble ourselves regardless of our experiences or our professional titles. Even at church, we think that we can jump in and take the pulpit to preach, but when the church asks for someone to clean up the bathrooms, or teachers are needed in the children's ministry, we ignore it because it is not the position we are looking for. We can't climb a ladder in one big step from the bottom to the top, it is impossible. Let's not forget that Jesus, the Savior of the world, said that He came to serve, and He washed His disciple's feet (Luke 14:11; Matthew 20:28; John 13:1–7).

We were experiencing a lot of supernatural miracles, yet physically I was still suffering. The symptoms in my body became worse. I was 88 pounds at this point. I was having anxiety and panic attacks more often than before. I even started to hear voices in my head that were telling me that I was going to die. The worst part of all this was that I was believing it was God telling me that I was done here on earth. I would sit on my couch, thinking about the five members of my family who died, including my brother who just passed away, and immediately think that I was the next one to die. I had no peace. I was afraid of everything. I couldn't even tell my own husband the battle I was fighting in my mind. Fear is a killer, and the devil knows when and how to torment you. Remember, I was bound by fear because of a past that took all the sources of security from my childhood. And now, I unexpectedly lost five members of my family in less than three years. I just had two babies in two consecutive years and now I had health issues. It was the moment, the opportunity for the devil to manifest what he had been rooming in my mind. I allowed him to go along with his game by entertaining and magnifying his evil and destructive thoughts of death. Because I didn't know how to face my giant, I did what was easy to do–ignore it for years, hoping that it would go away, but instead it found many opportunities to grow bigger and bigger (Romans 12:2; 2 Corinthians 10:3-5; Colossians 3:2).

I can tell you the exact day the devil planted his ultimate seed of fear in my mind. It was that specific day. I was very young and curious about everything. Some members of my family practiced witchcraft. They were very involved in this type of thing and I, out of my curiosity, started following them. I was not satisfied with my present life. It was hard to understand why I couldn't find someone to love and care for me. As I said before, I wanted to know my future, so one day I walked into a psychic's home searching for answers. She told me three specific major things that were going to happen in my life. I believed her at that time. What is so amazing to me is that, for some reason, I didn't remember this until the moment that the attack on my body came, which was the third thing that she told me was going to happen. It was here that I realized that the first two things she said were going to happen, already did happen exactly as she said. Here was the moment of truth. Who do I believe? What this woman told me was Satan's plan to one day wrap me into his web of lies to destroy me with a weapon that he knew I was running from. I couldn't face it–and that was fear. The first two things that she told me were major positive milestones in my life that happened, which was God's plan because all good things come from God, but the third one was bad (James 1:17).

Can you see the enemy's plan? His strategy was obvious, but not for me during the time it was happening. When this came to my mind, I ran like a dog with its tail between his legs. I was afraid like never before. I thought the devil had me and was going to kill me. This is what witchcraft does to an individual when we mess around with this type of stuff. The devil doesn't care if it takes years, as long he knows he has you, and then little by little you are feeding that lie to make it grow. He will use it at a specific time to destroy you.

I was forgetting that I have a covenant with God and that I am born again, that my past was buried. Satan, the liar, was bringing it back to me and making me accept it and receive it. He also has a plan for me–to cut me off from the face of the earth, so God's plan won't be fulfilled in my life. Does that tell you why? Because God's plan in my life will expose the work of the enemy. But I was a baby Christian, I didn't know better, and Satan is a bully. He abuses the innocent and the ignorant and he always tries to destroy covenants. You may be thinking, but when you got saved you were completely redeemed. My answer to that is, my spirit was, but not my mind. That had to be renewed (1 Chronicles 10:13; 1 Samuel 15:23; Leviticus 19:31).

Fear was controlling my thoughts and instead of running to God, little by little, I was running from God. I opened the door to confusion and to a religious spirit to come in and fill up the gap–the emptiness in my life. I did not realize it, but I was doing what the Israelites did when Moses took longer than they were expecting to come down from the mountain. They became very rebellious. They even built their own god to worship–a golden calf. They were doing the most detestable thing in the eyes of God–worshiping idols (Exodus 32).

At this specific time, a very good friend of mine called me and confessed to me that she was divorcing her husband because he was having an affair. I honestly couldn't believe it. I always saw these two like two love-birds, always loving each other, their family, and their God with all of their hearts. This really shook me. I didn't see that coming, and I was so disappointed about it (1 Samuel 16:7).

One morning, I was in my living room praying and I brought this situation to God. "God, I can't believe this man did this to his wife, he is terrible." Right then, God interrupted me and said, "He did it to a human being, you do it to me–your God," and pointing at a picture hanging on my wall, he said, "There is your god."

It was at that moment that I realized that I had put a man, my own pastor, on a pedestal. Yes, I had a picture of him on my wall. I didn't realize that the way I saw and thought of him was as if he was my god. I can't even begin to tell you how disgusted I felt. I admitted that I was worshiping a man. Sometimes we easily and unknowingly remove God from His place in our lives and we replace Him with something or someone else. The one who is immediately aware of that is the one who pursues us to replace God. The one who is ready and waiting for that to happen will take advantage and mess around with our minds.

We need to be careful of that. We need to check our hearts. The only way to do this is by looking at ourselves in the mirror daily– the Word of God. As you can understand from what you have read about me at this time, I stopped doing that. I didn't realize it of course, but my mind had been drawn into something else. I want to alarm you of this. Stay connected to the vine. Change and transform your mind daily. It's extremely important. I know many Christians who think that just going to church or reading a Bible verse here and there is enough; no, it's not. We must study, meditate, and live the Word daily. We need to be sober-minded and alert because our enemy, the devil, is going around looking to see who he can devour (1 Peter 5:8; John 15:5; 1 Peter 5:8).

The panic attacks continued. They were so bad that I thought I was having a heart attack. I would put my kids in the car and drive around the neighborhood, crying, thinking that I was dying. I didn't know what to do, where to go, or who to tell. My mustard seed of faith, my joy, and my peace were being robbed. No matter how spiritual I thought I was, or how much I knew the Word, when this attack came, it shook me. Every attack in my life has been different. I honestly thought that the biggest attack was losing my brother, until I was attacked in my physical body that came accompanied with a terrible fear of death. I had a weapon, and I didn't know how to use it (Ephesians 6:17).

Imagine you have a weapon in your hand and two robbers enter your home to rob your possessions and you do nothing but stare at them because you're paralyzed in fear. This is exactly what happened to me. Years ago, in Honduras, I worked for a clothing store, and the owner showed me a gun under the cashier box, just in case one day the store was robbed. Well, it happened, and I had my hand on the gun, but I was shaking. I couldn't use my weapon. Fear took place and I did nothing, I was paralyzed with a powerful weapon in my hand while the thief took over and stole whatever he wanted to, right in front of my eyes. My reaction to this spiritual attack was the same. I was paralyzed with a weapon in my hand (the Word of God) and not only that, but my peace, joy, and my health were being robbed right in front of my own eyes (2 Corinthians 10:4).

This tormented me. I called my husband at work many times, screaming to him, "Please pray for me," trembling in fear of death. Shawn found me many times sitting on our bed, staring out my window thinking of my funeral. This was devastating. I didn't know how to face or fight this fear that was taking advantage of my weakness each day (1 Peter 5:8).

One Saturday, I was looking for clothes to wear to church the next day. I realized that I needed a pair of black shoes to go with my outfit, so I went to the store and bought myself a cheap pair. I came home and found my family watching a movie that almost gave me a heart attack–for real. They were watching "Christmas Shoes." What a coincidence! A movie where a little boy goes to buy a pair of shoes for his momma who is on her deathbed. He wanted her to wear them to go meet Jesus. I kissed my husband really quick and ran into our room crying and tightly holding the bag with the pair of black shoes in it. I was seriously thinking that this was real, that I was going to die. My heart was pounding as if it wanted to come out of my chest. I heard loud voices in my mind screaming, "Get ready. Get prepared. It's happening soon."

I threw the bag with the shoes in my closet, wishing I had never gotten them. I was being tormented by a false sign that was not only taking my breath away, but my life. This was serious. I was dealing with crazy demonic spirits. The enemy of our souls will find ways of confirming his false alarms and accusations. Sometimes I thought I was fighting with death itself in my own strength. You may be thinking that I was losing my mind, and honestly maybe I was. That was one of the reasons why I couldn't share this with anybody because I didn't want to end up in a psychiatric hospital. My question is, how much can we take in our little heart? How much can our mind bear (Luke 22:31–32; Proverbs 27:12)?

Satan was taking advantage of my pain because he saw me going after God's heart and using my faith to see miracles, signs, and wonders. He wanted to stop that because he knows that my call is to show the world that God is real and if that is possible, then people will believe in the existence of a powerful God who works miracles. This will bring a revival of souls to the kingdom of God, and to Christ Himself, who is, who was, and is to come. Satan doesn't mind when we play church and be like little lambs, but when we choose to turn the world upside down for the kingdom of God, he does everything in his power to stop us. But God gives us power to overcome all the power that the enemy possesses. We just have to know how to use it (Acts 13:22; Hebrews 11:6; John 4:48; Luke 10:19).

Our wedding anniversary was approaching, and Shawn was planning for us to celebrate this time better than the year before when we had to stretch the only $7 that we had. God did it for us in a way we never expected. Let me share this story. We loved a place in town where they sold soups and sandwiches. Shawn, as a good husband, said, "You order your favorite soup and we'll share the 6-inch sub," and that's what we did. We had enough money to also order one cup of coffee (God knew, the man had to have his coffee). Shawn realized that the cup had a sticker on it for us to scratch off to win something. We won a doughnut! Yay! The server brought us the soup, and it was the wrong soup. That one was Shawn's favorite, not mine. I told her that wasn't the one I ordered, but that it was ok, and she said, "No. I'll bring you the right one." She looked at Shawn and asked, "Would you like to have it?" Yay! And that's how God stretched our seven dollars. He is faithful in all of His ways. I just want to clarify that this place was a coffee shop, no tips necessary. The server brought the soup to us because it wasn't ready at the time we ordered. We believe that as Christians we must bless exceedingly above and beyond those who serve us in restaurants (Proverbs 3:5).

My clothes weren't fitting me anymore because I was losing so much weight and I wanted to wear something nice to our anniversary celebration, so I thought to ask Shawn for it. At that moment, I heard the Lord saying, "Why are you going to ask him? Don't you know what's in the bank account? Ask Me. I am your Father." I realized that He was right! Why should I even ask Shawn when I knew that we didn't have the money for this? Why put another burden on my husband's shoulders? I knew that our season at that moment wasn't great financially because, again, I agreed to God's call in our life to go to the bible college and it wasn't easy, but it was just a season (Romans 5:3).

I trusted God with this, as I had no problem believing Him for material needs. I knew God as my provider, and a week later, very late at night, someone knocked on our door. I couldn't believe it; it was one of my friends from church. She came with a gift and she said, "I have been very disobedient, I had this gift for you for a long time. I have been so busy, but today the Lord prompted me to bring it to you." When I opened it, there was a gift card from my favorite clothing store (Psalm 23:1–4, 6)!

Finally, our anniversary day came, and we went away. We were very excited about this day. Shawn kept motivating me and trying to help me get out of that depression by doing different exciting things together. Everything was great, until Shawn left me alone for a moment, and immediately I felt this fear come upon me again and whisper, "Enjoy it because this is the last time." By the time Shawn was back, all the fun was gone. I began to pull away and put all kinds of excuses for us to stop enjoying our anniversary celebration. All I wanted was to run back home to my dark and quiet room to cry and feel sorry for myself. My mind began to fight the thoughts of panic. I was catching my breath and trying to hide the feelings from Shawn. It was as if my body was there, but my mind started to run miles away without turns or stops, but this time, and for the first time in front of my husband, I began to shake and I started to cry. Shawn was so surprised. He asked what was wrong (Revelation 12:9).

I was afraid to speak out. I was fighting all of this alone as I had opportunities to speak to Shawn about it before, but I couldn't. I don't know how to explain that I was afraid to even tell him. I was concerned about many things, one was of me losing my mind because I thought that no one else dealt with these things, and by losing so much weight, I thought that it was true that I was dying, and I didn't want to face that fact. This is crazy. That's exactly what the devil wants. He is a bully. He isolates you with his lies. One thing I can say is, this type of spirit will not manifest or torment you when you are around people that you know, but the minute you're alone, he isolates you not just physically, but in your mind. You are not able to think right. Finally, I was bold and confessed to Shawn what was going on. He encouraged me and took authority over this spirit by praying for me. We had a wonderful anniversary time considering my battle (John 10:10).

Shawn brought me to the doctor and found out that I was having acid reflux and a hiatal hernia. They prescribed medication. I was so disappointed because I thought that medicine was against my faith. I really thought that I was doing something against God, and that I was losing my faith. I thought that miracles only happen in a supernatural way, so taking medicine for me was contrary to that. Also, a dear sister in Christ tried to confirm that to my heart. She came to my house and asked, "Where is your medicine?" I showed it to her, and she said, "God told me to tell you that you need to throw it away." The blind leading the blind. I wish I knew how to use the Word at this time and would say, "Get behind me, Satan." Because if she was the one staying up many nights seeing me suffer in pain and rushing me to the emergency room in the middle of the night, seeing me having trouble swallowing, then she probably would force me to take that medicine. But thank God for my husband Shawn, who had faith in the supernatural power of God, but still insisted that I must take my medicine, so I did. It helped but I was still having symptoms. The doctor decided that I needed surgery. This scared me even more. I was taking medicine against my will and now surgery (Matthew 24:4; Matthew 16:23)?

What's so amazing is that before this challenge came to my life, not only did I criticize the people who had surgery, but those who were always at the altar looking for prayer for healing. Now I was one of those in line at the altar. It's easy to criticize someone until you're in their shoes and feel their pain (Matthew 7:1–5).

I won't blame anybody but myself for all of this, because my view of healing was distorted. I was spiritually raised in "Pentecostal" churches, where emotions are used a lot. I have been in services where I saw people getting up out of their wheelchairs, people being healed instantly, and that for me was the "only" way God works. What I didn't know was the before or after life of those who got healed at the altar until I had a conversation with a friend of mine who got healed of her vision problem in one of those long, emotional church services. She told me that after the service, her husband gave her the car key to drive. He was excited that his wife was finally healed and now she could see perfectly without glasses. However, she was so nervous because it wasn't true. She was not healed yet but chose to fake it. She was driving and crying afraid to have an accident, so she took out her glasses and put them on. She now had to go to the stores hiding herself from church members who came to her to congratulate her for her miracle. She didn't want people to see her using her glasses because she celebrated in front of the church and proclaimed being healed. What went wrong here (Ephesians 4:18; Hosea 4:6)?

Healing miracles happen and they are true, I know that for a fact. Many people have had the same experience as my friend; she received her healing at the moment in the service, but she didn't know how to keep it. If we all read the Bible and understood it, we would realize that healing is real and it can happen instantly, or with time. The Word of God was sent to heal as many as would believe. It's OK to stand in faith with the Word, proclaiming it until its complete manifestation. Those of you who take medication, do not lose hope or faith. Medicine helped me very much with the symptoms, and it didn't make me less spiritual. It made me painless and I was able to swallow and sleep a little bit more. I thank God for that good gift. He truly guided my steps. If you can suffer the pain and stand in faith believing the Word, I take my hat off to you out of respect, that's awesome (Proverbs 22:3)!

God wants us to face our fears, not to run from them. David faced Goliath. Daniel faced the lion's den. After drinking spiritual milk for so long, the time came for me to consume meat, whether I liked it or not. When I was a child, I talked like a child, I acted like a child. It was time for me to grow up spiritually (Joshua 1:9; Hebrews 5:12–14)!

The moment of the surgery came. My faith was shaking again. What happened? I'm definitely losing my faith, I thought. Once again God used my husband to speak reality into my heart. I cried, telling him that I was afraid to go through the surgery because, in my understanding, it wasn't the way God works. Shawn explained to me that sometimes it takes more faith in God to go through the surgery, to lay on a table in the hands of a doctor, believing the Great Physician will sovereignly guide the surgeon's hands, than to believe for an instantaneous healing. He continued, "Remember when God created the woman? He put Adam to sleep and opened his side and took out a rib. Then He closed Adam up and woke him from his sleep. What do you call that?" "A surgery," I responded. Exactly! Even God is in the surgery business. He gives doctors wisdom. The way he explained it to me brought me peace. Thankfully, I had the surgery, and everything went well (Even though, after the surgery, the doctor told me that the surgery wasn't necessary, that everything looked great inside, but he was already in, so he did what he needed to.) In other words, he removed my gallbladder even though it looked great and healthy. After all, he was just trying (Genesis 2:21–23).

All of this may sound confusing to you, but it's because, when you suffer from a sickness, you have to make sure no one tells you what to do. It's your body, you hear from God, let Him direct you. This is very important. Always keep your eyes on God. Trust him. Trust His Word regardless if you are taking medication or having surgeries or not. God is the only one who can heal us. God uses whoever and whatever He designs to bring healing to our bodies, but I am still a big believer in the supernatural healing power of God through His Word (1 Peter 2:24; Psalm 103:1–22).

It amazes me how God guides our steps and connects us with the right people. I remember one day I walked into church and right at the door a lady saw me and obviously realized that something was going on with me because I was only 88 pounds. She grabbed me by my arm and jokingly said, "Girl, the wind is going to blow on you and take you away," and she continued walking. Another woman took some time to hear my pain, and said without hesitation, "There's a spirit of death in your family and it needs to be rebuked." Do you want to know where I ended up that day? In the hospital! My issue wasn't just my physical body, but it was my mind. I was fighting a spirit of fear and their words weakened my resistance against it. I didn't know how to bring my thoughts captive to the power of Jesus. The Bible says that we should encourage one another, so if your words are not doing that, then please know that your silence will be more helpful. Let me stress that again. We need to be mindful of our words and the way we speak to one another. Your tongue can build up the faith of your friends or unwillingly be used by the enemy to harm and discourage your friends. Use the discernment of God. Live by the Spirit. Unfortunately, wherever we go we will find the same types of people. We have to remember that we are commanded to owe nothing to anybody but "love" (Hebrews 3:13; Proverbs 12:18; 18:21).

All of this was a training field for me. My whole life continues to be just that–a learning experience of my walk in Christ. As a Christian and someone who loves to pray and encourage people, I learned so much during this critical time in my life. One day, we were in a prayer meeting at our church and the leaders asked if there was someone who needed prayer, to raise their hand, so again, I didn't miss an opportunity of letting people pray for me. That's how desperate and afraid I was. Never forget this when you see people always asking for prayer. You never know what their motives are; for me it was the fear of death. I raised my hand and one of the leaders came and asked what I needed prayer for. "Acid Reflux," I said. She hit my stomach with her hand so badly that I felt my esophagus jump. I didn't know what to do. I honestly didn't see that coming, and she kept pushing her hand deep into my stomach. I remember looking at Shawn trying to ask for his help. In any other situation, this would be considered a physical assault! I had no other option than to fake that I was falling down under "the anointing" as some people do under the power of the Spirit. That way she would let go of my stomach. It was a wise move because she did. I left that prayer meeting with so much pain not only in my stomach but feeling guilty in my heart because I lied. I went home and I shared with Shawn how I felt and as always, he encouraged me not to feel bad, that I did the right thing. My intention was not deceptive but to protect my body from this woman's aggression. Please, when you pray for people, keep in mind that they may be in pain, or weak, or afraid. The power of God doesn't manifest less or more because of the way you pray, or the tone of your voice, just pray the Word in Jesus' name (1 Peter 3:8)!

Don't misunderstand some of my negative experiences with well-meaning church folk. I also met some wonderful women. There were those who God sent to my path with a significant purpose. Warriors that know how to fight the good fight of faith. I want to mention a specific one. She stood out in the crowd for one reason and one reason only, she walked like Moses with the presence of the glory of God all around her. That caught my attention. I can tell you that this woman knows her God. It was evident to all. I went to her and asked for a couple minutes of her time. She gave me her address and asked me to come to visit. I was desperately waiting for that day and time. I couldn't even sleep the night before, thinking, or I should say, having a long conversation with her in my mind, telling her my whole list of issues as we cried together. The next day I walked into her house and she totally surprised me. "Get on your knees right now and talk to your Father," she said. I did what she asked as she threw a prayer shawl over my head and left the room. Immediately, I was in His presence. I cried and cried, asking God for help. Minutes later, she came back and gave me a list of Bible verses on a piece of paper and instructed me to study and meditate on them, and then kissed me goodbye! I was disappointed. "That's it?" I thought as I went home. Honestly, I read the Scriptures she gave me here and there and out of all of them, only two stood out and stuck in my mind. They were Philippians 4:8 and James 4:7. That's all that I needed. The Word of God carries His power. I remember thinking and thinking of these two Scriptures over and over again. They would just come to my mind. God watches over His Word to perform it (Jeremiah 1:12).

That same week, I had a visit from another prayer warrior woman of God. A friend who could discern what I was going through. I was in bed, sick. She knew that she was there on a very important assignment and with Shawn's permission she walked into my room. She sat on my bed and said, "Glennys, this is going to be weird, but I have to do it. Come sit on my lap." I obeyed her and she held me as a mother holds her child. She began to pray for me, rebuking the rejection, pain, insecurity, and fear that I was carrying since my childhood. She spoke the Word over my life, and I felt loved and protected. That day, I slept in the peace of God (Galatians 6:2; John 13:34).

The following week, another friend surprised me with a visit. She walked into my house speaking in tongues and asked for a large bowl and towel. She filled it up with water, put the towel on her shoulder and began to wash my feet. While I was in tears releasing my pain and fear, she spoke the Word of God over my life, sang worship songs in the Spirit and then left (Proverbs 11:25).

All of these experiences blessed me. This is gold to me. To know that there are people who hear the voice of God and are not afraid or ashamed to act and do whatever He tells them. It's a tremendous blessing for me and it should be for you. This is the reason that I can't ever dismiss the voice of God when He asks me to do something–to go on a mission. These things can change, transform, and rescue a life. Being there for someone when they need it the most, representing Christ's hope of glory by humbling ourselves to show others that mercy says, "No, I'm not going to let you go because you were born with a purpose." It's priceless. The obedience of these three women opened my eyes and helped me to break through the hands of my enemy. This is why it is so important for us to live by the Spirit, hearing the voice of God, and following His instruction. We are commissioned to go and not just to preach the gospel, but to heal the sick and to set the captives free. To do what God is calling us to do is humiliation for some, but for others, like me, it's gain (Mark 16:15; Matthew 10:8; 1 Corinthians 1:18).

About a month or two later, I had another incredible visitation from my best friend! I was in my room, sitting on my bed, sewing a button back onto my husband's shirt when the needle fell from my hand onto the carpeted floor. I began to carefully look for it without success. I was afraid that the children would walk into my room barefoot and get hurt. I continued looking for it but could not find it. I sat on my bed again and asked, "Jesus, please put that needle in my hand." I believed in my heart that He could and was about to do it. I didn't say, "Can you please?" I knew He could. I asked, "Please put that needle in my hand." Believe what I am about to say. Immediately, I not only felt His presence, but I heard His steps walking on my carpeted floor. I closed my eyes very tight as I automatically knew that my natural eyes weren't allowed to see Him. I couldn't believe what I was experiencing at that moment–Jesus Christ, the son of God, was about to perform a supernatural miracle right in front of my eyes. I could feel Him right next to me as I bent down with Him grabbing my hand and putting it right where the needle was. I grabbed it, and I began to cry so deep. Still with my eyes closed, He said, "The same will happen with your health, if you believe." I was amazed by this experience. I wanted to share it with the whole world. I lay on my floor, crying, thanking Jesus for being so real to me. My only desire that day was to have opportunities to tell the world that Jesus is alive and that He does miracles. I felt my heart pounding so hard at that moment because of the experience I just had. I even thought that no one would believe me because these things are viewed as impossible, but all things are possible for those who believe. I believe with all of my heart that Jesus is still a miracle worker (Deuteronomy 10:21; Jeremiah 32:27; Luke 18:27; Exodus 15:26).

Later that night, when my husband came home from work and the children were already in bed, I grabbed my Bible and told them not to bother me. I walked to the basement with my heart determined that this day was going to be the day it all stopped. I was going to face my giant–this fear once and for all. I was determined that this was the day of my death, or the day of my freedom. I threw myself on the floor, crying, "God, I can't live life with this anymore. I can't live one more second, hour, day, or month suffering. God, if I'm going to die, then let it be now, but I can't anymore. Please answer me. I need you, Lord, please!" (Jeremiah 33:3).

Suddenly, I heard a voice behind me loud and clear. "Come to me. You're running miles away from me. Come. Come to your Father's lap." It was Him, God. He was sitting on my husband's prayer reclining chair. As His sheep, I recognized His voice immediately and got up and sat on the chair. I felt His arms around me. I had my Bible open on my lap and automatically I began to flip the pages when a wind came out of nowhere and began to flip the pages faster and faster and stopped right at 2 Timothy 1:7, "For God did not give you a spirit of fear, but of power, love, and of a sound mind."

I cried inconsolably, but this time it wasn't because of fear, or due to a panic attack. It was because the truth opened my eyes. I stood up and faced Satan, screaming, "If it wasn't God telling me all of these things, that I was going to die soon, that I would be the next member of my family to face death, then who? Who did this? Who was telling me these things? It was you, Satan, you are a liar. You have been tormenting me, but today I submit to the Spirit of God, I resist you and you must flee from me. It's over. You came to steal, to kill, and to destroy, but Jesus came so I can have life, and more abundantly." I cried tears of joy in God's presence. I worshiped Him and He continued ministering to my heart with His Word. Perfect love casts out fear. I carried this fear and many insecurities from my childhood. It was a seed that was planted in my heart and I was never able to face it or deal with it, but instead I hid it and gave the devil a foothold. He knew the exact time in my life to use it to destroy me–but God (John 8:44; Genesis 50:20)!

I have been free since that day, but the Bible is clear, when a demon comes out of a person, it goes and finds seven bigger and returns to the house he left. If he finds it empty, he stays there, and the condition of that person is worse than before. Now, it's easy for me to recognize when he tries to come back. Therefore, I make sure that he never finds my house–my heart–empty. When God told me that I was running miles away from Him, it was true. Going through all of these situations, instead of running closer to God, I ran further away from Him. I have no explanation why, other than I needed to stay connected to the vine at all times. I can't afford to assume that not having daily intimacy with God is normal, or that He'll understand. He promised that He will never leave me, and He never has, but He can't promise that I will never leave or disconnect myself from Him. That's my free will (Matthew 12:43–45; John 15:5–7; Hebrews 13:5).

Before this physical attack came, I was attacked in countless other ways and I fought the good fight of faith and saw the victory, but when my own body was attacked, I couldn't fight because I didn't know how. I felt weak and I was afraid of dying. This is when fear became very real to me. I didn't know how to really face a giant, or how to be strong when I was physically weak. I knew how to fight for others but not for myself, and the enemy knew that. I did what Samson did. I gave my secret away. Samson told Delilah the secret of where his strength came from–his hair–and Delilah cut it off. I gave the enemy my joy, the secret of where my strength comes from, and he cut it off. As Samson, cutting his hair not only took his strength, but his vision–his eyes were taken out too. It was the same with me, not only that my joy was gone, but my vision–the reason why we came to Columbus, Ohio, and the plan and purpose of God in my life. I forgot all of that, but instead I thought that everything was over. But it is not over until God says it's over (Judges 16:1–31).

As we served in leadership at our church, we attended many prayer meetings, but there's one specific meeting that stuck with me forever. I believe it was the first time that someone taught me to pray the way we prayed that day. That someone is our pastor's mother (Titus 2:4). There was a group of female leaders from the church having a prayer meeting. We were sitting in a circle praying quietly, when she walked in and very loudly asked us, "What are you all doing?"

I picked my head up and looked at her thinking, how can she do that? We are praying! She asked the same thing again and this time even louder, "What are you all doing?" and then she began to scream, "Get up, get up. Is this the way you're going to the enemy's camp?" she asked. "Is this how you take back what the devil stole from you? Is this how you think you'll take back and fight for your children, your marriage, your finances? Is this how you fight for your health?"

She began to speak in tongues and laid hands on all of us. She was speaking with so much authority and power! I remember her laying hands on me and screaming, "Fire!" I got it that day. The impartation was so strong. We prayed and we knew that things were done and that we got everything back into our hands. I went home, still under that anointing (1 Timothy 4:14). I kept telling Shawn how powerful it was. I believe that day something new was born inside me. Prayer and intercession were awakened in me. Please don't misunderstand me, I'm not saying that you have to pray loud or long for God to answer you or to be powerful in the Spirit. I know that you just have to agree with the Word of God and use it with authority, but for me, at that time, I needed this impartation. I needed to see and experience everything to understand it better and be able to say now that I am who I am because of my process of learning and growing spiritually. I have experienced prayer in different ways and levels and with different people from different denominations and their ways of praying. This has made me understand what unity really means. I'll explain more in another chapter of this book (Ephesians 4:1–6)!

I know that God is not looking for perfect people to use. That truth alone should make us all grateful. He is looking for obedient vessels. But one thing I can say is this, you can be changed and transformed through the process–if you allow Him. He is the same yesterday, today, and forever. He does not treat one person differently than another. He wants us all to walk in our complete healing and wholeness physically, spiritually, and mentally here on earth. That is what Jesus died for. He didn't die in vain. He paid the price of our punishment for our peace, our joy, our healing, and our salvation. We need to receive it all as a gift (Hebrews 13:8; Romans 2:11; Isaiah 53).

He wasn't going to leave me the way I was. Little by little, God was pulling out the roots that were deep in my heart. Remember, coming from a past like mine, there were a lot of unbiblical thoughts, traditions, and hurts that had to go. Honestly, I believe that there's more. He is never done with me. I depend so much on His love, goodness, and mercy, but one thing I can say is that I'm not where I would like to be, but I'm not where I was years ago. He is faithful. He is real (2 Timothy 2:13)!

When I became a Christian, I remember asking Him to break me in pieces, like His vessel, and put me back together again the way He wanted me to be. He was doing just that, but there was more than one thing that was hidden in my heart (Hebrews 4:13). I know He is faithful to do with us as we ask and allow Him. As for me, I was desperate for change and hungry for His Word. I wanted to see His will fulfilled in my life. I didn't know the cost, but I wanted it. I was tired of the life I was living. I was tired of being a slave of Satan. I wanted to be a servant of the Most High God. He wants us to live a life that represents Him here on earth. He wants us to live to the fullest in His joy and purpose. Keeping pain hidden in my heart prevented me from experiencing my complete healing. Remember, God doesn't do half-baked miracles, or bring you halfway on a journey and leave you hopeless. He always finishes what He starts in us. He is not interested in using you more than what He is truly interested in–transforming you for His glory (Romans 12:2)!

Let me tell you about my little secret. No one knew. I couldn't talk about it because it brought guilt, shame, and condemnation.

That was the abortion I had before I met Shawn. I knew that God forgave me, and I had no issue with that, but for some reason I avoided thinking about it because the thoughts were very hurtful to me. The only people who knew I had this abortion was the man who was responsible for it and the abortion clinic in Union City, where I had the procedure. I thought that no one needed to know and that I didn't need to talk about it, so I unsafely buried this secret deep in my shattered heart. But the reaction of that pain was impossible for me to hide or bear. Every time I saw a baby, or I heard about abortions or miscarriages, I felt guilty and condemned by my sin. How could I erase this painful past? My silence wasn't working, instead it was more hurtful to me (Romans 5:3–5).

One night, as we were asleep, our oldest daughter came to our room crying, "Mommy, I can't sleep." I ran to help her, and she hugged me tight, telling me about the dream she had. "I saw babies without heads, feet, or legs." Just while she was saying this, our oldest son came running to our room crying, "Mommy, I had a bad dream." Shawn and I asked him what his dream was, and he said, "I saw babies without heads, arms, or legs." This really shocked me! I couldn't even keep listening or comfort my children. I asked Shawn to take care of it while I ran to the bathroom to hide from my own guilt and condemnation. Shawn prayed with the kids and put them back to bed (Jeremiah 15:18).

When Shawn came back to our room, I was crying so much that I couldn't keep this secret from the man who loves and cares so much for me. I confessed to him about my painful secret. Honestly, that wasn't too difficult at all. My past has never affected Shawn. He has always been quick to forgive and move on. We prayed together and went to sleep (Ephesians 4:32).

I woke up the next day, thinking how easy that was. Now not only does God forgive me, but also my husband. I thought that was it. I'm free! But I continued hearing people talk about abortions and the guilt and shame kept resurfacing. Hearing or thinking about it was still painful.

Time went by and once again, in the middle of the night, both of our children, who slept in different rooms, ran into our room, screaming in fear. They both had the same dream where they saw babies being cut into pieces. I couldn't help it, but I started to cry, tormented about this painful secret that somehow was materializing after years of being buried in my heart. These repetitive experiences with our children's dreams brought me back to that day, that moment of the procedure. I began to feel regret. Why did I do this? Why didn't I keep my baby? I felt this conviction and knew that no matter what I did or who I would tell about it, the pain wasn't going away. Once again, Shawn handled it very well. He prayed with all of us and then he prayed for me and we went to sleep (Genesis 3:10).

That same weekend at church, our pastor began to talk about something that God was calling him to do. He was opening a women's pregnancy crisis center in Columbus, Ohio. After making the announcement, he did an altar call. "If you ever had an abortion, or if you're a man who ever brought a woman to have one, run down to the altar," he said.

I looked at Shawn and shook my head—no! Like saying, I'm not going there. I felt the embarrassment and shame coming out. While a lot of people walked to the altar to be delivered, my flesh was fighting with my spirit and thoughts of confusion were overflowing in my mind. "What will people think of me? What will my pastor think of me? No one knows this little secret. What if they think this or that? But I want to be free." At that moment, I heard God asking me, "Do you want to be free?" Right there, I knew that was my moment. I needed to move quickly and allow God to do the work in me. I let go of my reservations and walked to the altar. My pastor looked at me and said, "Be free!" (Isaiah 54:4; Galatians 5:1).

I wish I could say that that was it. But no, after that, we were sent
to a room to put our names on a list to start attending a "Post-
abortion bible study." Here is when my healing started. I was so
excited about this. I remember that the first class was on a Thursday
evening. Our teacher was an amazing and strong spiritual woman
of faith. She asked us to one by one introduce ourselves and share
our story. I wasn't the only one suffering this pain, shame, and
condemnation. I believe there were more than fifty women present
at this initial bible study. Everyone's abortion experience was
devastating. But there was one woman from another country who
really touched my heart with her story. "I was very young when
I got pregnant and my mother brought me to have an abortion. In
my country, they don't use anesthesia, so it was extremely painful.
I was screaming and my mom grabbed me by my arms, the nurse
by my legs, and the doctor with a knife performed the abortion, but
I didn't do this just once. I did it two, three, four, and five times. If
I got pregnant, I knew what to do," she said, as we all cried with
her (Matthew 5:7; Hebrews 4:16; Jeremiah 1:5).

At the end of that class, the teacher asked us if we knew the sex
of our baby or babies. I personally thought that she was out of her
mind when she asked that. I think she realized that the expression
on my face was telling her just that, so looking at me she said,
"Girls, pray and ask God to reveal it to you." Are you joking,
I thought? Yes, me, the faith-walking lady. I believe that God can do
anything, but I thought that this specific thing, "asking God for the
gender of our babies," was unnecessary. I shared my opinion with
another woman and she seriously encouraged me to pray about it
(Psalms 127:3; Isaiah 43:1; John 10:3).

On my way home, I kept talking to God about that specific thing.
During that week, I took time to continue asking God for it, but
nothing happened until the day of the next class. I was driving my
kids to the library that afternoon. It was a beautiful, sun-shining
Thursday. I can point to exactly where I was turning at that moment
when this happened. I was making a turn and all of a sudden the

sky turned dark and started to thunder, and once again, my ear turned very hot and together with a loud voice mixed with thunder I heard, "Esmeralda!" (Emerald) I couldn't believe it. I started to cry, oh my, oh my–the baby was a girl. I continued driving, but less than a minute later, the storm stopped, and the sunshine came back out. It was like the storm didn't even happen. I was astonished by the whole thing. This is how important our heart, our deliverance, our freedom is to God. He wants us free. He knew that this was tormenting me. We can come to Him with filth in our hearts, but it's not His desire for us to stay filthy and to live life in bondage. He is our deliverer. He is our freedom, but we have to receive it (Isaiah 49:1–26).

I got to my class and the teacher asked, "Did God reveal the gender of those babies?" I was so excited to tell my experience how God revealed to me not just the gender of my unborn child, but her name. What was more fascinating to me was that most of the other ladies had a unique or similar experience. God was working in all of us together for His own purpose. I couldn't give what I didn't have. I can't put into my heart God's life and Spirit and not have a reaction from His holiness cleaning and purifying my heart (Psalms 51:1–2).

The class finished that day and as I was about to leave, the teacher looked at me and asked, "Glennys, what's Esmeralda's last name?" That's it, she ruined everything right there! I looked at her and felt as if lightning was coming out of my eyes to strike her. I asked, "Are you serious?" "Yes," she said and continued saying, "Let me know next week."

I walked out of the building very disappointed. I felt as if I was being shaken by a strong turbulence. My friend and I drove together that day and almost got into an accident because something very mysterious happened. It was pouring rain, but we could assure you that there was a man lying on the ground and that we almost hit him.

I was so upset I thought that this was my last day attending the meetings. I wasn't coming back. I was so rattled because my teacher was stepping on my toes. Now she was digging up deep roots. In my own mind, she was bringing up my painful past. Bringing up my sin. Bringing up my mistakes. I thought that she wanted me to give her the last name of the man who hurt me and, honestly, I wasn't ready for that. I thought that she was wrong for doing that. I believed that she needed to stay on the surface, but she was going too deep and it was very uncomfortable (James 4:8).

Finally, I got home and went to lay next to my husband. Very quickly, I fell into a deep sleep. I heard God asking me in a dream, "When you married Shawn, did you have two or three children?" I responded, "Three." God continued asking, "Did he adopt two or three?" Immediately, I woke up and then woke Shawn up and I asked, "Shawn, when we married, did I have two or three children?" He said, "Three." I asked him, "Did you adopt in your heart two or all three?" And he said, "Of course I adopted all three of them." Right there, I said, "Esmeralda Hyland!" (Ephesians 5:25–26).

I couldn't believe what was happening. God was working my way out of this painful secret that for years tormented me. Shawn and I were amazed at everything that God was doing, not only the physical miracles, but the spiritual healing in my heart from my painful past (1 John 1:7; 1 Peter 2:14).

Early the next morning, I decided to clean up my closet. I was sitting on the floor organizing my shoes, when I saw something rolling so I grabbed it. It was a loose ring that my sister had given me years before. The ring had three big green gems on it. Then it hit me. Wait, this is what "Emerald" means. I ran to the computer and I Googled the name, "Emerald." The first thing that came up was a ring like mine with a big green gem. I started to cry. Right there, God said to me, "As that ring, Esmeralda was lost for you, but now she is found." I threw myself to the floor and cried and cried, not even realizing that I was squeezing a cloth I had in my hands. I heard Jesus say, "Who touched me?" Those inner words made me cry even more because those are the same words Jesus said when the woman with the issue of blood touched the hem of His garment. "" Who touched me? Because strength came out of me" (Luke 8:45–46). I couldn't stop crying, thanking God for His faithfulness and His love to deliver me and set me free. Now I was ready to tell the whole world that I was free and forgiven (John 8:36)!

I went to my next class and told my story to everyone, especially my teacher. I didn't even wait for her to ask for Esmeralda's last name. I looked at her with a big smile on my face and for the first time, I felt something inexplicable. It was like Heaven kissed Earth when I said it. "Esmeralda Hyland." Since that moment, I accepted my reality; she is part of me. She is my child, a human being who is in Heaven and one day I'll see her. From that moment on, I didn't have to keep her as a mystery, as my mistake, or a hidden secret of my past anymore. I'm not ashamed of my past because I know that Jesus paid the price and set me free!

After this bible study, I was trained to be a coach at the church's Women's Center in Columbus, Ohio. I volunteered there and God used me to save many babies. I was on a mission and I told Satan, "For that one life that you stole, I will save many more." And that's what I did. I remember one specific young woman who came, thinking that we were an abortion clinic. I was in a room talking to her and she was telling me that she was confused. She didn't want to have an abortion, but she was afraid of the future and especially of her parents. I ministered to her heart, gave her some important information that she needed to know about an abortion procedure, and offered her an ultrasound just to make sure everything looked good inside her womb. She accepted it. At the moment of the ultrasound, she requested me to be in the room with her and I agreed. When she heard her baby's heartbeat, she opened her eyes so big and asked, "What's that?" The nurse told her that it was her baby's heart and she started to cry. She looked at me and said, "I'm keeping my baby. I won't have an abortion." What's so funny is that the moment she said that, the baby on the ultrasound screen stretched so quickly and gave us a thumbs up–literally! All of us, including the mom, laughed so loud. This has stayed with me forever. I'm sure that it also has stuck in that young woman's heart forever too. Thank you, Jesus, and thank you to my pastor for your obedience to open that clinic and giving me the opportunity. What an awesome God I serve.

We continued our walk with a miracle-working God!

R eview–Fear is a killer. My biggest mistake was to live in denial instead of facing this giant. The battle in my mind was intense. Instead of running to God, I ran from God. Fear manifested itself in the weakest and most painful moment of my life. I removed God from the place He belonged in my life. After that, I found myself worshiping idols. I had a powerful weapon but did not know how to use it against the enemy of my soul.

E ncouragement–Face your giants. Do not be afraid of fear. Expose the lies of the enemy. Deal with your issues. Do not let them grow bigger and bigger because Satan can use it to destroy you.

A pply–2 Timothy 1:7; Isaiah 35:4; 41:10; 54:17; 1 John 4:18; Philippians 4:6–7; 2 Corinthians 10:4–6; Ephesians 6:10–18; Psalm 23:4; 34:4; 56:3; 1 Peter 5:6–7; John 14:27; Matthew 6:34; Romans 8:31–39; Philippians 4:8; Luke 10:19; Hebrews 4:12.

L earn–I learned that the thief goes around like a lion looking to see who he can devour, and that when a demon comes out of a person, he goes and finds seven bigger demons and tries to come back. If they find the house emptied, swept and cleaned, they stay there, and the condition of that person is worse than before. I learned to use my weapon by staying connected to the vine at all times.

Chapter 5

My Greatest Lesson Learned!

We continued seeing miracles in our lives. All of these experiences were good for us and even more for our children. To see them growing in their faith, trusting, and believing God for everything in their lives was amazing (Proverbs 1:8–9).

What do kids do when they see their friends' new toys? They want them, right? Our children started to ask for a Nintendo. Sadly, we did not have the money for it. As parents working hard to provide for your children, the inability to buy your children the things they desire is humbling and heartbreaking. But I knew who could provide their desires. I told them to pray and ask Jesus for it, that He was the one who could give it to them. Train a child in the way he should go (Proverbs 22:6). That same week, we took our trip to the grocery store (Yep, I went food shopping with four children–not easy). I remember having two on each side holding onto my clothes; they weren't allowed to let go of my shirt. I had the other two in the shopping cart and sometimes I packed that cart so full that you couldn't see them. That specific day, they wanted some yogurts, and they picked the ones that come in individually wrapped skinny packages inside a box. The packaging marketed a promotional contest to win a free Nintendo. The odds inside later revealed there was one winner for every 10,000 boxes. They picked a box, we finished shopping, paid the cashier, and went home. They trusted in the Lord with all of their little hearts (Proverbs 3:5–6). They were so excited to open that box! It was as if they were 100% certain that they brought home the winning box. We quickly opened the box and took out all the yogurts to see if the winning message was inside. We noticed that one package was empty. At first, I thought it was a mistake, that the manufacturer forgot to fill it in, then I realized that there was a piece of paper inside. I couldn't believe it. While opening the empty package, my hopes that this was the winner started to rise up. My contained enthusiasm was right. They picked the winning box! Yes, they got their Nintendo. Come on, who does these things? Who? Other than our God the Almighty! We must become like little children trusting in His promises (Matthew 18:3).

Later on, we didn't have the tuition money for our children's Christian school, so we decided to homeschool them. I know they wanted to go to their school instead of being homeschooled, but we sat with them and explained the financial situation. Again, I told them to pray and ask Jesus, that He could do it for them. Of course, I also prayed for this and the very first day of school a lady from our church called me and asked, "Why didn't I see your kids at school?" I explained to her and she said, "I'll call you back." She called me back right away and said, "Not only is their tuition taken care of, but their lunches are paid for the whole year too. You just have to put them on the bus." What's impossible for God (Luke 18:27)?

We met a lot of good friends at church. I can truly say that they weren't just friends, they became family to us. We were always helping and encouraging one another. Among those friends was a young lady. She was a bible college student who walked miles every day to attend school because she had no car or money to buy one. One early Saturday morning, after coming from the store, she came to my mind. Right there, I heard the Lord say, "You're driving her car." I understood exactly what God was trying to tell me–I was supposed to give her my car. I knew this would be difficult to explain to my husband. I began to make a "deal" with God. "If that's you, Lord, then let Shawn say that it is OK," I said. When I got home, Shawn was asleep. I woke him up and asked, "If God tells us to give that car away to that bible college student who walks every day, would you give it away?" Without hesitation he answered, "Yes."

I have to admit that deep in my heart, I was so excited about this. I was never able to give away something this big–a car! Even in the middle of my financial situation, it looked as if I was the one who had more need than anybody else, but God was asking us to be a blessing, and honestly, it was for a reason. I needed to learn to obey God, not only when He asked for little things, but also when He asked for big things. I learned that it is not the size of the gift, it is the obedience of our hearts. In Genesis 22:1–19, God asked Abraham to give Him Isaac, his only son. Not only did he obey, but Abraham trusted God and expected a good outcome. I don't know about you, but for me, it feels so much better when I give than when I receive. I felt incredible to be able to give a car away.

I called the young lady and invited her for dinner. She came and while she was eating, I put the key next to her plate and told her, "That car that is parked outside is yours." She went crazy! She grabbed the key, saying, "No way! No way!" She cried and told me that the same week, she planted what, for her, was a significant and sacrificial monetary seed in obedience to God. She gave not out of her abundance, but out of her heart, believing for her own car. She was now able to move around without difficulty. About a year later, we went to Washington, DC, to see "The Call" with Lou Engle's ministry. We were seated in the street when I immediately recognized that car. Yes, it was her. She drove all away from Columbus, Ohio, to go to the same event we were attending. That was amazing. God is awesome. All for His glory!

The Lord also blessed us with a beautiful house. Even though we went bankrupt years before, we were still able to buy our house. Our heart was to use it to bless others. We had people over all the time. The idea of hosting prayer and intercession groups grew bigger and bigger in my heart. I knew the power that is in prayer and I was excited to do it in my individual life, and with others in corporate prayer. I knew that prayer works, and it became my biggest desire to see people calling upon the name of Jesus in prayer and intercession (1 Timothy 2:1; Matthew 18:19–20).

With our church leaders' permission, I started to host a women's prayer meeting at my house. I didn't know that this is when my ministry, or I should say my calling, started. I asked every woman to bring one thing to the prayer meeting, whatever they felt in their heart. Just one thing, like a bag of bread, or a package of diapers. I was very specific that they weren't allowed to go shopping for this—no spending money. It was whatever they already had at home, if they had something. This wasn't a mandatory thing; they could attend even if they didn't bring anything. I will have a basket at the door for them to put what they brought into the basket. I told them that at the end of the prayer meeting if they saw something in that basket that they needed, then they could take it home, and if any of them needed the entire basket then the whole basket was theirs. I had so many testimonies about this. The idea of this was to bless one another. That basket became a blessing to many. If there were any left-over things, I would find people, such as bible college students with a need, and allow them to help themselves to our basket of goods. God is our provider (Philippians 4:19).

One specific lady was going through a lot of financial issues and couldn't even afford to buy a bottle of shampoo. She came to the prayer meeting that week and found not just a shampoo in the basket, but her favorite expensive shampoo. Another lady needed diapers for her baby. She was in a desperate financial situation, but the Lord supplied her needs. She found her baby diapers in the basket also.

We became more connected spiritually and it helped us to fight our battles together as one body. It's so amazing that after many years, I still receive messages from some of the women, saying how much of a blessing this was in their life. When God gives you one simple idea, never overlook it because it looks insignificant in your eyes, just obey because in the end, what looks like a drop of water becomes a river of blessings. My God will meet all of your needs according to the riches of His glory in Christ Jesus (Philippians 4:19).

Remember that at the same time miracles are happening and you see the hand of God moving, you also will have trials and tribulations. Of course, the devil will use anything and everything to stop the work of God, but that's his job and he does it very well. Just make sure that he doesn't distract you or stop you from accomplishing what God called you to do. Do your job and do it to the best of your ability regardless of the opposition.

I remember one night after our prayer meeting when the ladies were leaving. I said goodbye and while closing my door I heard gunshots–boom, boom, boom, boom! In seconds, someone knocked at my door. It was some of those ladies, they were running for their lives. They came inside and we realized that it was my next-door neighbors. They were a very young couple with two children. The police came, no one got hurt, but since that moment I began to pray specific prayers for those neighbors. One morning, early in the morning in prayer, the Lord said to me, "Go to your next-door neighbors and tell them that 'I AM' sent you to pray for them." I didn't hesitate. I knew that I was hearing from God and for Him to say, "Tell them that 'I AM' sent you," that was enough. I learned from the story of Moses in Exodus 3:1–12, that there was no need for me to fight against the "I AM" command. I knew that the same way He protected Moses and His people, He was going to protect me and my family. Actually, I was excited because I believed that He was about to do a miracle that would let His people go, so they could go worship Him. I love to see God perform miracles, to see people changed. To bring souls to the kingdom was a desire that was growing bigger and bigger in me.

I showed up at their door. I knew they were drug dealers and they had guns, but I also knew that I was sent by a powerful God–the

I AM, and He was with me. I knew I heard God give me these instructions. I knocked on their door with so much confidence. The wife opened the door and I said exactly what God told me to, "The I AM sent me here to pray for you guys."

She went crazy. She started to cry and called her husband, "Babe, Babe, come." Him, holding his pants up and shirtless, ran to the door and said, "What's up?" And I repeated to him, "Hi, the I AM sent me here to pray for you guys." And he also went crazy, "What? What, Babe, what? Oh man, this is crazy." They both were crying. He walked back and forth in his hallway crying until he could finally talk, "Babe, tell her. Tell her what just happened." She said, "We both were Christians. My father is a pastor, but we don't go to church anymore. We walked away years ago, but this morning, right before you came at the door, we were talking about our lives and we decided that it is time for us to go back to God ... and that's when you knocked." They couldn't stop crying. They rededicated their lives to Christ. I prayed for them and I left.

I couldn't stop thanking God. That was just unbelievable. Hearing the voice of God and obeying and doing whatever He asked me to was just amazing. I continued praying for that family and we blessed them as much as we could. They went back to church for a while, but then the drug situation got out of hand again, so I had no other choice than to pray for them to get out of the neighborhood. Less than a month later, after I began that prayer, there was a big U-Haul truck, and they left (John 14:13).

There have also been times of disobedience in my life of course. I remember one time I was volunteering in the children's ministry at my church. One Wednesday night, while I was taking care of the nursery room, a little girl was crying and feeling very uncomfortable because of a bad diaper rash. It needed Desitin cream to soothe the pain and make her feel comfortable. Even though the cream was right in front of my face, I chose not to do it. I was too tired to pick her up and take care of it, when another volunteer called me from another room about my own daughter and said, "Glennys, your daughter is having a bad rash, is it okay if I use some Desitin to make her feel better?" I couldn't believe it. This made me think of the Scripture that says, "Do unto others what you will like others to do unto you" (Matthew 7:12).

Another time, we had no money for food. All we had was a package of chicken in the freezer. I woke up early in the morning and, while preparing the chicken, I heard in the inside of my spirit, God giving me instructions on what to do, just like in the story of Elijah and the widow at Zarephath in 1 Kings 17:7–16, God said to me, "Cook that meal and bring it to this specific family."

The family He wanted me to bless with this meal was going through a lot. They are a very large family and, at that time, the wife was pregnant and about to give birth. But instead of obeying God instantly, I began to reason why I should cook my last package of chicken and bring it to someone else? What about my own family? And what will we eat, nothing?

I cooked the meal, and yes, I served my family not theirs. We were seated at the table and about to start eating, but my conscience wasn't leaving me alone saying, "You're about to eat your seed. Don't do it." While Shawn blessed the food, I was struggling and I wanted to yell, "Wait. Please don't eat it. Let's not eat our seed." But at the same time, I thought it was too late, that I already made my decision, and at that moment, our phone rang. Who do you think it was? You won't believe it! Yep, that family. The husband called desperately asking us to please watch their children while he went with his wife to the hospital; she was ready to give birth to their child. What a relief for me. I immediately said, "Yes." They came and we all ate the meal together. What a God we serve! He knows our hearts and our struggles, and not only does He give us instructions, but He also helps us to accomplish them through opportunities so we can be blessed (Psalm 1:1–6).

I want to clarify that I don't believe that God will punish me if I don't obey Him. No, the point is clear that what God wants is for us to be blessed. Like in this case, I believe that He wanted to multiply my seed, but it was my choice to eat it. I knew that in my own conscience, that's why I was struggling with my decision. But was God going to punish me like an angry father with His daughter that didn't obey him? Of course not. My decision of disobedience closed the door of multiplication–the blessing. But even after all of that, God's mercy and grace was sufficient. Once I recognized that I was wrong and that I was making a wrong decision, he helped me make it right. It's clear that he doesn't make decisions for us. It's our own choice. Our own decision–choose today whom you will obey or follow. As for me and my family, we will serve the Lord (Joshua 24:14–15).

We gave God both of our lives and He was instructing and training us (Proverbs 3:5). At this time, God started speaking to our hearts about our own ministry. Before Shawn came to me and told me what God was speaking to his heart, I already knew it because He was saying the same to me. Normally, this is how the Spirit of God operates in our lives (Jeremiah 33:3). That was a big confirmation for both of us. So, we started to work behind the scenes getting prepared in obedience to God. We grew eager about this as if we wanted to see the whole thing done immediately, but we needed to control our emotions. Personally, I started to think big as I always do.

Shawn shared with me the name that God gave him for our ministry. Psalm 99:1, "The Lord reigneth; let the people tremble: he sitteth between the cherubims; let the earth be moved." MOVE THE EARTH. This was the perfect name; we are called to move the earth for His glory. We kept all of this in our hearts and on paper.

We continued living life as normal, but now something didn't feel right. It was as if we weren't comfortable anymore. We wanted more. We wanted to be used by God in a different way, but this is when we needed to remain faithful and be still (Psalm 46:10). A lot of things happened at this time. Many of our friends moved back to the state where they came from or to a different state. People that I never thought would move away were gone. However, God continued preparing us. We officially incorporated our ministry and had everything ready to go, but we were waiting for God to release us. Everything was done step by step.

Why is it that most of the time when God calls you to do something great and exciting, He tells you, shows you, anoints you, and then you have to wait? And the worst part of it all, according to our human view and emotions, is that there's something to do in that period of waiting that is not pleasing to you, even if it is to do what you have been doing for years. Who wants to slow down when your emotions are all hyped up? But we must wait and obey God. Do everything according to His time and in His way, or it won't work. For example, God sent Samuel to anoint David, the shepherd boy, as king, and right after that, David didn't go and take the throne. No, he went back to the sheep (1 Samuel 16).

Sometime later, I woke up from a dream in the middle of the night and realized that Shawn was up working on something. I went to tell him my dream and to our surprise, he had been up making my dream a reality. I dreamed that we were both wearing a T-shirt from the ministry of the church we attended at that time, but God handed us each a T-shirt with our own ministry logo and told us that it was time to take the old ones off and put on the new ones. That night, Shawn, without telling me anything, was working on ordering T-shirts for us with our ministry logo imprint on it–Move the Earth! Who needs more confirmation than that (Luke 8:17)?

At this time, Shawn was still a staff member of our church. Three years later. he graduated as the valedictorian at bible college with a 4.0 GPA (*I want to put this here because I am extremely proud of my husband because he worked hard for this, sleepless nights, three different jobs, waiting lines in food pantries to feed our kids. I just want to give honor to whom honor is due. You did it, my love!*). We continued praying and asking God for direction and wisdom on how to do what He was calling us to do. We knew at this point that it was time to go back home. Yes, He was sending us back to New Jersey to start our ministry. I remember praying for this many times and each time I prayed for New Jersey, I felt heaviness, toughness. It was as if we were going to a dry and hard land. I kept pushing in prayer and finding encouragement in the Word. God showed me a lot of things and a lot of people that we were going to meet for a purpose—a divine connection. Amazingly, He even showed me some people that we needed to stay away from. I wrote everything down, told Shawn about it, and kept everything in my heart (Jeremiah 33:3).

At this point, we knew the name of our ministry and where we were going, but one thing that was extremely important to us was to leave on good terms with our pastor and leaders, so we waited to be released. Honestly, this was hard. I thought we were ready and there was no reason to be held back, but God is a perfect God, a God of order. Even though our hearts were more excited for the future than connected to the present, we continued serving and being faithful to our house of worship. "Let not steadfast love and faithfulness forsake you; bind them around your neck; write them on the tablet of your heart" (Proverbs 3:3).

We had many confirmations that what we were doing was the right thing. This is what God was calling us to do. One day, our pastor's mother preached a strong message about being obedient to God, and she specifically said, "Do whatever God is calling you to do. Go wherever he is telling you to go. If he says go to..." she sort of paused. Then she said it, "to New Jersey, then go to New Jersey." I couldn't believe it. Shawn and I, we looked at each other like, Wow! How did she know? Where did that come from? What a big confirmation. She could say to North Carolina, or to Florida, but she said, New Jersey.

And if that wasn't enough confirmation for us, later that month, a preacher came all the way from Africa as a guest speaker, and when he was preaching that day, he walked down the aisle and pointed at

Shawn saying, "God is calling you out and you need to go." That was it for us. We seriously began to get ready to move back.

Later on, Shawn was called to a meeting where the church was laying off a lot of their staff because the church couldn't afford them due to a loss of a lawsuit and a national economy that was in recession. This was our moment. We shared with our leaders about our ministry and all of what God had been putting in our hearts, and all that we had been working on behind the scenes in obedience to the voice of God. They prayed for us and released us to go and do our mission (Galatians 5:22).

Finally, the wait was completed! We sold our house to a family from our church and called all of our friends to come that Saturday to get whatever they wanted (free) from our house. We were ready to go start our new beginning. Yes, we once again gave everything away. I knew that we needed to plant seeds, because we would need a big harvest. Within days, everything was gone. We put our clothes and our children in the minivan that we purchased by using the car that the lady from the deli department at the grocery store blessed us with years ago as the down payment. We began to take the road to the next chapter of our lives. Everything has a purpose (Psalm 57:2)!

We said "goodbye" to a lot of friends that were "family" to us and we were on our way to New Jersey. It's amazing the way God works in our lives. Everything happens for a reason. What's even more amazing is that most of the time we have no clue of God's plan, or the things and the people He uses to guide us into the right path. Remember how God released my heart from the bitterness, anger, and unforgiveness I was holding against that person close to my family? Well, for us to move back to New Jersey we had no other option than asking this specific person to let us live with her. She had a four-bedroom, two-level house for her and her mother alone. I honestly felt humiliated by this, but because of our children we had no other option. This situation right here makes me think of how important it is for us to live at peace with everybody because we never know who we will need one day. On the other hand, it makes me think that's the reason why Satan brings discord to put us against one another to destroy God's plan. He knew that one day I would need help from this person, and he was trying to do his best to block that door, but God used it for me and my family's own good (Proverbs 4:23).

What an experience we had on our way to New Jersey. We prayed and prayed in our van. At one point, the Lord showed me a bridge that was far away in front of us and He asked, "Do you think you'll pass over that bridge?" I had no question about it, I was so sure that we were going to pass over that bridge and without hesitation I responded, "Yes, Lord, it's on our way." We got closer and closer and to my surprise, I realized that we did not pass over the bridge. From one point of view, faraway, it looked as if that bridge was in front of us, but when we got closer, it wasn't. That bridge was far away to our right side. That called my attention and that's when God said to me, "The same thing will happen with you in New Jersey. You will think that you're going in one direction, but it will take a different direction than what you think." I shared this with Shawn, and we kept it in our hearts. "For my thoughts are not your thoughts, neither are your ways my ways," declares the Lord. "As the heavens are higher than the earth, so are my ways higher than your ways and my thoughts than your thoughts" (Isaiah 55:8–9).

We finally arrived in New Jersey. Once again, we were sent by God and had nothing, no money, no jobs, and not even our own place where to lay our heads to call home. Yes, the owner of the house sent us to the basement. She probably said "yes" for us to live with her out of pity and love for our children, but she was not happy to have us there. I understand now. We weren't just two people. We had four children and no jobs to help her with the demands we were bringing into her house. She had always lived in that big house with her mother, no noise, no children running around, so to still keep her peace, she sent us to her basement.

Here we were, about to start a ministry, sent by God, and living in an old basement. There was mold in some areas, even bugs like the huge crickets crawling around us at night while we slept. We went to a Catholic church to ask for blankets to lay on the floor together with our four children. We felt as if we were homeless. We applied to many different companies, looking for a job but found nothing. One thing that the basement had was a "bar" in a corner, where this family and friends would drink and play cards, but for me, that corner became my "secret place." Who would have thought that the physical secret place where I met with my Savior, Jesus Christ, would be a "bar" one day? Every morning, I was at the bar seeking God's presence, and It's there where God spoke the most to my heart. For my thoughts are not your thoughts, neither are your ways my ways!

As faithful children of God, we had no doubt that we were to attend the same church we attended before we left for Ohio, and we did, but to our surprise, things weren't the same. What had happened to our beautiful church? We could feel something in the atmosphere, and we started to find out that a lot of people had left the church. What is so funny is that we would see some of those people at stores or at restaurants, and we were so excited to see them. We would run towards them to say hello, and they would turn around and walk away. This confused me. What was going on? What went wrong? We weren't even here when the church had an internal problem. These people were so hurt or angry with one another that, because we were attending that church, they saw us with the same eyes they saw everybody else who attended that place of worship. Honestly, we didn't even know any details of the situation. We never asked, never wanted to know. We just wanted to love our brothers and sisters, but an enemy came during those years of our absence and planted a bad seed that grew bad fruit that infested many hearts (Matthew 13:24–48).

Later, we found out that the church suffered a split. Meanwhile, we remained there and continued to be homeless. Things started to get harder and harder for our family. I finally got a job in a deli department at a store in a local community. I ministered to so many people there. A lot of people received Jesus as their Lord and Savior, and I shared all my experiences with God to many of my coworkers. Shawn was still looking for a job. He applied to many different companies, but no one called him. At the same time, he started to work on our ministry, and that began to succeed very well.

One thing that was like scales coming off of my eyes was that I would talk to Christians about all the miracles that God did and was doing in my life as a normal conversation. I thought all Christians experienced God the same way I do, but to my surprise, they would literally look at me as if I was out of my mind. I began to realize that Christians weren't experiencing the same miracles as I was. Sharing my experiences with the Lord was like shining a bright light into the darkness. I was waking them up to the realization that there's more. It was as if for the first time they heard, in person, someone who experienced resurrection power. It was as if they just met a celebrity. For me, I was just experiencing the God of the Bible. I'm not kidding! That was like an arrow that penetrated deep into my heart. I couldn't understand how they didn't have anything to share. Why did people have no stories like mine to share? I honestly felt bad. What happened to Christians that are not living like heaven here on earth? I met so many Christians at my new job and told them my testimonies. They were astonished! When I discovered this, I was driving home from work one day and I was bawling my eyes out to God, telling Him, "They don't know who they are or even who you are." This was so painful to me, because I discovered that not only did I need to share the gospel with unsaved people and bring them to Christ, but now I had another mission, and it was to encourage my brothers and sisters to look for more. I was like the woman who found her lost coin. It was here that I realized that my call was more than just bringing souls, but to "Tell EVERYONE I get in contact with that GOD is REAL!" Since that time, I began to feel the need to lift up my brothers and sisters, encouraging them and praying for them. Fan into flame the gift of God (2 Timothy 1:6; Matthew 5:16).

The time came for our children to go back to school. Our biggest desire was for them to attend a Christian school, but how? How could we afford a private school for four children?

One day, as I was praying at the bar in the basement for this specific situation, I heard two biblical words that God dropped in my spirit. I thought He was encouraging me to trust Him. That morning I shared with Shawn what God told me, and that's when Shawn said, "There is a school here with that name." And right there everything made sense.

We decided to go to the school just to see it. We got to the administration office and spoke to a sweet lady who gave us all the information about the school, including their tuition prices, and right there I thought it was time to go home. I explained to this lady our financial situation, she got our information, and we went home. In our car there was silence, and when we got home, I threw the papers away. That's impossible, I thought (Luke 18:27).

In the middle of the night, I ran to the bar again, not to drink, of course, but to talk to Jesus, and I told Him my disappointment. "All that we have is a deli department job, how can we afford that school?" And right there, He said to me, "I had a situation like that one." Immediately, I said, "You, you had a situation like this one?" And He responded, "Yes, remember when I only had five loaves of bread and two fish to feed the five thousand?" (Matthew 14:13–21).

I felt as if someone just turned on a light and lit up the entire room. With excitement, I answered, "Yes, Lord." And He said, "Do what I did." I grabbed the Bible and quickly I began to read this story and there it was, He looked up to heaven and prayed!

Yes, I can do the same, I thought. Just look up to heaven and pray and that's what I did. My unbelief got out of the way and I realized that it was time for a miracle. I put my faith to work. I trusted that God was going to make a way for this because He said it (Jeremiah 1:12).

Early that morning, I got a phone call, it was the principal of the school. I remember his exact words as if I was hearing him right now. "Hello, Mrs. Hyland, my secretary told me that you and your husband were here yesterday. She also told me about your situation and out of the list of children waiting to get into the school, God told me to choose yours."

I literally almost passed out. All I could think was, "You did it, God, you did it." We went to meet with the principal that same day. On our way there, God spoke to my heart. He said, "You are not only going to receive a blessing, but will be a blessing. They need a Spanish teacher and I want you to work one year for free to bless that school."

This probably does not make sense to you, like it didn't make sense to me at that moment. We were struggling financially, sleeping on a basement floor and He is asking me to work in that school one full year for free. This reminded me of when the blind man came to Jesus asking Him to give him his sight back, and Jesus spat on the ground, made mud, and put it in the blind man's eyes; then asked him to go and wash it in the Siloam river. It doesn't make sense, but this man's obedience healed him. He could just get discouraged and say, forget this, I am going home, but instead he followed Jesus' instructions and that opened the door of his blessing. I did the same. We went to our meeting and they offered us an amazing discount for our children's tuition. Honestly, we were still not able to afford that insignificant amount, but we took the offer. We were done with our meeting when I was bold to do what God asked me to do. I asked if they had a Spanish teacher and the principal answered, "No, are you a Spanish teacher?" I responded, "Yes." and immediately he opened a drawer and took out a contract and said, "You are hired." I explained to him my mission with this and it was hard for him, but he accepted. I volunteered in that school for one year and at the end of that year I found out that they were closing the school. I didn't know what was next for me or for my children. Where do we go from here? God always has a plan and purpose for each of us, we just have to trust Him and not our own understanding. In all our ways acknowledge Him and He will make our path straight. (Proverbs 3:5–6)

That weekend, I was invited to a prayer meeting that a church in the area was hosting. I attended and at the end as I was leaving, I grabbed a pamphlet and realized it was from their school. I asked the lady behind the visitor's desk, "Do you guys have a school here?" She answered, "Yes, do you have children?" "Yes", I said. "And I am a Spanish teacher." We continued our conversation and while she was talking, I heard in my spirit, "Give her your name and phone number." But I thought, No, that would be weird, and I didn't; instead I walked away. I was about to leave the building when I heard behind me, "Excuse me, Ma'am, Ma'am." I looked back and it was that same lady. "You're going to think that this is weird, but can you give me your name and phone number? Just in case we ever need a Spanish teacher," she said. I immediately gave her my name and phone number. If we allow the Holy Spirit to guide our steps, we see the glory of God in our life and in the lives of our loved ones! Always keep this in mind, whatever decision we make (good or bad) will affect not just us, but those around us–our loved ones (Psalm 32:8; Philippians 2:3–4).

About a week later, they called and offered me a job. What an opportunity! Who would have thought that my obedience to volunteer one year without taking a salary in another school, in the middle of a difficult financial situation, would bring me to the right path? This was a blessing not just for me, but for my children's education also. I ended up quitting my job in the deli and started my new position at this school, where my children also started attending that next year.

I want to encourage you to always obey the voice of God, regardless of your circumstances or the way your present situation looks. Always remember that His ways are better than ours. Believe me that most of the time, when God tells me to do something, it just doesn't make sense to me, but I learned not to walk away and do my own thing to mess it up, but to be extremely careful to follow His instructions–and it works. My family and I have lived the life of miracles. Always walking not by my might, not by my power, but by His Spirit (Zechariah 4:6). Thank God for His clear guidance in our lives.

A lot of things happened during this time. Shawn was still without a job, but he was growing our ministry. He did amazing events on the beach, spreading the gospel and bringing souls to the kingdom, and overall speaking out loud the truth of Christ. We did MTE's Jesus Shore event, which brought the attention of the national media and Shawn was invited to the FOX News Fox & Friends News Show. I clearly remember that day. They came to pick up my husband in a luxury car with another pastor to bring them to NYC for the interview. I was so excited to see him on national television telling the world what God was doing in our region. And there we were, our children and me, gathered around the TV, sitting on the basement floor. How ironic. He came back from being on the number one cable morning news show in America, to his family in the basement. He was tired from the early rise and traveled into the city and came home to lay down on the floor to take a nap.

 But we didn't lose hope. We knew that God sent us here and that we were doing what He called us to do. Once again, can't you see that sometimes things look like they don't make sense? But when you recognize the voice of God and you know that it is Him walking you through, you're confident, regardless of the wind that steers the waves that rise up during the storms in your life. The disciples didn't recognize Jesus at first when they saw Him walking on water in the middle of the storm. Whatever spirit you are, get away from us, they said. But when they heard, "Take courage! It is I. Don't be afraid." Right there, they knew that it was their Lord and Savior. They got so excited that even Peter asked to be called to walk on water (Matthew 14:22—33). This is exactly how I felt when I found out through the reading of the Word that Jesus is a miracle working God. I wanted to be used by Him so desperately. I wanted to be called to walk on water and have faith like Peter, and now I'm able to say that It's real. God is real.

During this time, God continued to change my heart. He is never done with me. I learned that I will never arrive until I get to Heaven. My human heart gets in the way sometimes, but the spirit that's alive in me helps me in my weakness. In my conversations with Shawn, he told me once or twice, "My love, I think that you need to have more grace for people." That really bothered me (Please, keep in mind that most of the time God will bless and speak to us through people, especially those close to us–so never dismiss when your spouse or your own children bring something like that to your attention). Everyone should be quick to listen, slow to speak, and should not get easily angry (James 1:19). In my first week working in that other school, they told me that I needed to do a personality test on their computer, so I did. At the end, I wanted to hide.

The results, in my understanding, didn't match my personality. I thought something went wrong, maybe the computer did something wrong. I got a result similar to this:

Compassionate (✓)

Missions (✓)

Giver (✓)

Helper (✓)

Loving (✓)

Diligent (✓)

Grace (X)

That's when I realized that it wasn't Shawn telling me this, but it was God, my Father, trying to fix those things that somehow can affect my life and my walk with Him here on earth. I am the kind of person that I have asked God to do whatever it takes to change me–to mold me. One thing that I asked the most for was for Him to help me to walk in holiness. (1 Peter 1:16). I went home that day and I asked Shawn what that word "Grace" meant. He answered something very simple, "To give people a break." But to each one of us grace has been given as Christ apportioned it (Ephesians 4:7).

Since that day, I learned to be more careful about the way I see, think, and speak about any human being. You never know why people say what they say. Not everyone is trying to hurt me or offend me. I learned to give people a break! To be humble. "God opposes the proud but gives grace to the humble" (James 4:6).

Another lesson I learned at that time was the day I came home from work and my children were anxious, waiting for me to play a game. They explained the game to me and because I thought I knew my husband more than he knew me, I gladly accepted to play the game called, "Who Knows Who More?" I was so excited as I thought I would win and put my husband to shame. I was so sure that I was going to be the winner.

The children brought us individually to different corners of the basement and gave us two different papers with questions that we had to respond to. These are some examples of the questions:

Paper #1

1–Daddy's favorite color?

2–Daddy's favorite restaurant?

3–Daddy's favorite food?

4—Daddy's favorite place?

Paper #2

1–Mommy's favorite color?

2–Mommy's favorite restaurant?

3–Mommy's favorite food?

4–Mommy's favorite place?

Then they read the answers comparing what my husband said was his favorite things and what I said his favorite things were and vice versa.

Surprise!

His answers about me were all correct, but my answers about him were all wrong. They didn't match. The children claimed him as the "Winner" while I was boiling in anger and confusion. I couldn't understand.

Later on that night as we went to sleep on the basement floor, face to face to my husband, I was still holding the loss of the game in my heart. I whispered to Shawn, "Why did you lie? I always thought that was your favorite color, or your favorite restaurant, or food or place?" His answer was like a sword that pierced my heart. I ran to the upstairs bathroom to cry and to ask God to help me. Shawn said, "My favorite color is not brown, most of my shirts are brown because you bought them for me. It's your favorite color, not mine."

He continued, "We go repeatedly to that restaurant, not because it's my favorite, but because you love it. I do all these things and go to all these places not because they are my favorites, but because all that I want to do is please you!"

This truly changed my life forever. If we confess our sins, He is faithful and just to forgive us our sins and to cleanse us from all unrighteousness (1 John 1:9). I was wrong and I didn't even know it. I realized that God was still dealing with deep things in my heart that needed to be changed and transformed. My eyes needed to be opened and only God knew how to open them. Again, allow me to say that all of these things didn't make me feel like a victim. I asked God to help me to live a holy life, a life that's pleasing unto Him. My deepest desire was to represent Christ here on earth, for people to see that God is real, and He was showing me "Me" in my heart. Because of my painful past, I was trapped in my own prison–my mind and my thinking. To truly serve God,

I needed to die and truly walk in the new life that I have in Him. Walking at all times with a friend like Jesus has changed my life forever. Oh, what a joy it is to be called "Friend of God." It's not about me, it's about Him and those around me, my husband, my children, my friends, my coworkers. I want to light up the room when I walk in with the joy and the peace of God. To bring light to the darkness and salt to the earth. Healing to the broken hearted and the sick. Jesus is the answer for everything (Ephesians 5:8; 2 Corinthians 12:9; Mark 16:17–18)!

This whole thing made me think that the same way I thought I knew my husband more than he knew me; we are the same way with God. We are Christians, but do we really know Him as we should? This creates so much confusion in the Body of Christ (1 Corinthians 14:33). God wants us to know Him, so we can love Him for who He is. In the end it's all about dying. Dying to our own flesh. Jesus died for us and we need to die to our flesh in Him, so He can live through us. Christ wants us living a life that's heaven here on earth through Him. We are to put others above ourselves (Philippians 2:3–4).

Over a year went by and what humbling experiences I had. We were still in the basement and things started to get very tough for us. We wanted to see things change and we both were seeking God more and more and asking Him to help us. One day, Shawn came out of prayer and said, "It is time for a new beginning for us." It was that day that we decided to visit a church that we were sure would help us grow more in our walk with the Lord (Hebrews 6:1).

It was a Wednesday, and we were on our way there, and Shawn said to me, "God told me that we will find our provision here in this place." I added my faith to his and we walked inside the building. What was so amazing was that the pastor looked at us and he said, "Wow, we were about to contact you and you're here." When the service started, in praise and worship, I really felt as if I was home. I ran to the altar, crying and worshiping the Lord. What a release

I felt in my heart, not just for me, but for my family, our children. Feeling at home in my place of worship is very important to me because I don't want anything to hinder my worship and my spiritual growth. Even though, as in any relationship, things can get tough sometimes, or misunderstood, when we have a pure heart, we take courage and allow God to walk us through any situation by being humble, obedient, and faithful! Remember that when you are in a boat, the waves won't always be calm and pleasant, sometimes they will rise up in turmoil because we have an enemy, the devil, who hates spiritual growth and healthy, godly relationships. Be alert and of a sober mind. Your enemy, the devil, prowls around like a roaring lion looking for someone to devour (1 Peter 5:8).

At the end of praise and worship, the pastor got up and asked, "Who is that lady that ran here?" For a moment, I thought I was in trouble. Shawn looked at me and asked me to raise my hand and I did. How encouraging it was to me when the pastor said, "This morning, God told me that he was going to bring our worship to another level, and you ran here to worship, thank you for your obedience." (John 15:14) He started to preach his message when suddenly he stopped and asked his congregation, "Quick, Church, quick, get a seed in your hand. We are about to give the first good ground seed and God is telling me to give it to this young man." And he pointed to Shawn, saying, "God just told me that you came for your provision today." This blew our minds away–seriously! We still remember this as if it happened yesterday.

That next Sunday, we were there again, but this time with our children. Since that time, this became our home church, our place of worship. Our closure with our other church was bittersweet. We sat down with our pastor and he released us with a prayer.

Finally, Shawn got a job at this church. We were able to move out of the basement and rent a house. As you would expect, we would soon experience more miracles and more transformation in our hearts!

R eview–Reading the Bible every day and making my
relationship with Jesus a daily priority changed my life,
my thinking, and the way I see things. It activated my spiritual
eyes. Even though my faith is as little as a mustard seed, being
submissive and obedient to God makes me follow any instruction
He gives me regardless of the circumstances. Reading the Word
encourages my faith to trust God. What's insignificant for me,
might be significant to God. Obedience is better than sacrifice!

E ncouragement–Always remember that we are saved by grace
and that we need to represent Christ here on earth by loving
others with the same love and compassion that God loves us, and
overall to extend grace to others.

A pply–Ephesians 1:7; 4:23; 31–32; Matthew 6:9–15; Luke 6:27;
18:10–14; Psalm 32:5; 103:10–14; Proverbs 10:12; Romans 3:23;
2 Corinthians 5:17; Micah 7:18–19; Mark 11:25.

L earned–I learned the way forgiveness works best for my heart.
I must forgive others, but forgiveness had more of an effect
when I applied it the other way around–that is, I need others to
forgive me. This reminds me of the two men who went to pray at
the temple. The Pharisee prayed, "God, I thank you that I am not
like other people–robbers, evildoers, adulterers, or even like this
tax collector. I fast twice a week and give a tenth of all I get." But
the tax collector stood at a distance. He would not even look up
to heaven, but beat his breast and said, "God, have mercy on me,
a sinner." Forgiveness has more effect when we admit that we also
do wrong, that we are not perfect, and that we also need others to
forgive us when we do wrong. Keep in mind that God, who sees
everything, even the depths of our heart, is quick to forgive us and
remembers our transgressions no more.

Chapter 6

My Greatest Humbling Experience!

We were more than ready and excited to start this new chapter of our lives–it was a new beginning. Shawn was hired to work for the church, and at the same time I was volunteering in many different areas–facilities, children, food pantry, women, and the altar prayer ministry. At this point, our ministry, *Move the Earth*, was fading a little bit, but not from our hearts. We were giving our local church 100% of our time. We started meeting more people and I continued doing what my heart desired–encouraging and lifting people up in prayer (1 Thessalonians 5:11). This was a great season. We were able to move from the basement and rent a house. We were still struggling financially, but at least we were able to live on our own and pay our rent. I was still working part time at the school, which was a blessing to my family. A precious friend of mine from the school called to ask if I would like to take some furniture that she did not need anymore. We happily received it! Her furniture matched the house and was the exact style and color that we wanted. What a perfect God (2 Samuel 22:31)!

People were blessing us so much! Shawn's father gave our daughter a beautiful bed he had in his house, but we needed a truck to pick it up. Shawn asked a friend if we could borrow a truck from a store that he managed. The night before we went to pick it up, the children were sleeping, and Shawn and I were in our living room admiring everything that we had and thanking God for it. I said to Shawn, "For our house to be completed with all the furniture, I would like: (I was very specific, and I pointed to the specific spot where each thing would go.)

1–A brown headboard for our bed
2–Two small white bookshelves
3–A desk for Shawn to do the work of the ministry
4–A small hutch for our dining room

Shawn agreed with me and we went to bed. The next morning, Shawn went with our oldest son to pick up the truck first, which they left ready for him to use because the store was closed that day. Shawn realized that there were some things in the truck, so he decided to go to our house and empty the truck out first so he would be able to pick up the bed at his father's house. I was in the kitchen cooking when our son called me, "Mom, come quickly." I left everything immediately. I knew something was out of the ordinary because of the tone of his voice. Yes, I'm that kind of mother that can tell you each of my children's emotions by looking at them or hearing their voice or noticing their actions. I got outside and Shawn looked at me and asked, "My love, what was it that you said last night that you would like to have for our house to be fully furnished?" I repeated my list to him, and he said, "Look what's inside this truck." I couldn't believe it. It was as if someone was listening to our conversation that night and put inside that truck the exact things on my list including the size and colors of everything we wanted.

1–A brown headboard for our bed

2–Two small white bookshelves

3–A desk for Shawn to do the work of the ministry

4–A small hutch for our dining room

Immediately, Shawn contacted his friend, the manager of the store and his response was, "Someone went to get donations yesterday and didn't bring the things inside. They must have left it in the truck. I'm sorry." Shawn explained the situation to his friend and asked him to give us the price, as we would like to buy everything in the truck. The manager instructed us to take pictures of each piece of furniture and show it to them to see and confirm with the person who picked up the donations the day before that this was the furniture he left in the truck. We paid the amount they asked and did not even have to go find any of this. It came right to our door. This was just out of this world. God never stopped surprising us with His sovereign way of taking care of us. The Lord is my shepherd; I shall not want (Psalm 23:1).

God was doing amazing things in us and through us. I continued ministering to people with the gospel and sharing my stories. Some of our neighbors gave their lives to Jesus. I never stop using God's discernment and following His instructions. I wanted to be used by Him and to go into all the earth and spread His gospel. (Mark 16:15) This was my heart's desire.

One day, I was at a grocery store and somehow got into a conversation with a lady. I was telling her about Jesus dying on the cross while she kept searching for her produce items. She was listening and walking, but at that moment she stopped, looked straight at me and asked, "Who?" I paused and was tempted to have a "Peter's denial moment." (Luke 22:54–62) There were a lot of people around and she was about ten feet away from me, so I had to raise my voice a little bit or get closer to her and whisper my response to her question. I knew that I was about to mention the name that's above every other name and for some reason I was concerned about people's reaction. (Philippians 2:9–11) My boldness came out and I realized that I couldn't hide this truth, that it was an opportunity to speak it, so I said it, very loud, "Jesus Christ. He died on the cross for our sins." Literally, every person around looked at me. It was as if I just dropped a bomb. But the lady, she came close and asked more questions which eventually brought her to tears of real repentance. She received Jesus as her Lord and Savior! I strongly encourage you to be bold in this world with the truth of the gospel that sets people free.

At the end of a Wednesday midweek church service, I was still under the anointing of the presence of God. Right when I was leaving, I sensed that God was doing something. I couldn't tell what it was, but I was excited to see His Spirit moving. I started to run around the church building, yeah, like a crazy lady. I was shouting and rejoicing for something that only my spirit knew. After I did three laps, I went home. The next morning, I was teaching in the school to a group of international students. What a blessing this was for me. God always gives us opportunities to be used by Him. For no other reason than changing the cycle of having the students desks always arranged the same, I rearranged them in a circle, leaving the center open. This blows my mind away. I was teaching the bible class and all of a sudden, one specific student got up from his seat and started to run around the classroom in circles, shouting and saying, "I want Jesus. I want to receive Jesus!" I couldn't believe it. I stopped everything and realized that this happening right here was a manifestation of what I did the night before–glory! For everyone who has been born of God overcomes the world. And this is the victory that has overcome the world—our faith (1 John 5:4).

That international high school student got saved. While I was driving home that day, I heard in the inside of my spirit, "China came to you." Right there I remembered a dream I had months before. In my dream, I was sent to a specific community in China to bring healing Scriptures to a group of people infected with leprosy. No one could go there with the intention of preaching the gospel, so I ripped out pieces of my Bible with healing Scriptures and I hid them under my clothes. The military allowed me to pass through because I was going as a part of a medical group. I was walking in when a man came toward me. He was afflicted with leprosy.

I grabbed one of the pieces of a torn bible page under my clothes and gave it to him; he read it and immediately was healed. He then ran to bring it to the entire community. Some of the people afflicted came to me. Quickly, I took all of the pieces of the Bible with healing Scriptures and gave it to them. One soldier saw the whole thing. He was astonished to see the power of the Scriptures. One by one people were being healed, so he let me go. I woke up from my dream thinking that maybe, just maybe one day, God was going to send me to the beautiful country of China.

Fast forward to my class. Here I was being used with students from that country, but they weren't physically infected with leprosy. However, they needed healing in their hearts and salvation for their souls. Many students in this group got saved. What amazes me the most is they brought the Word with them to their own families in their hearts. I am commanded to let everyone I get in contact with know that God is real (Hebrews 4:12; Proverbs 4:22)!

One day, our daughter was invited to a pool party at the house of her classmate from school. We arrived there a little bit late, as we already communicated that to the host family a day before. We do not like to show up late for anything. Every human being on the planet deserves respect. In this case, respect for their time. When we finally arrived, all the other children were in the pool, and all the moms were talking and having fun. I realized that one kid was drowning, and I began to call everybody's attention. To my surprise, none of the adult "moms" that were there knew how to swim. No one could jump in and save this little boy. We were screaming and making a big commotion, but no one was helping. Suddenly, this little boy's sixteen-year-old cousin, who didn't know how to swim either, jumped in to save him, but now she was drowning too. We continued screaming like crazy ladies, panicking, but doing nothing else to help. Finally a brave woman, one of the mothers attending the party, decided to do something. She jumped in and went around through the edges of the pool holding onto it with one hand and trying to reach the boy or the girl with the other hand. She had no success, instead she ended up being in trouble too. This was a crazy and equally scary experience. All of this happened within seconds.

Finally, the man of the house came running, dived in the pool and rescued everyone. He took out the little boy and put him on a chair. I honestly thought he was dead. Honestly. He drank so much water that he was white and yellow. He wasn't responding and his eyes were glossy and unfocused, as if he was about to breathe his last breath. Everybody was screaming for help and his mother in desperation looked at me and screamed, "Do something! Do something!" I did what I could do at that moment. I gave what I had. I almost jumped on top of that little boy, grabbed him by his shoulders, and I screamed twice, "In the name of Jesus come back! In the name of Jesus come back!" Right there, at that moment, he was back. He started to cry, his color returned, water started to come out of his mouth, and his eyes were back to normal. His mom wanted to make sure he was back and asked him, "Who am I?" Crying in fear, he responded, "My mom!" Praise the Lord. Use the name that is above every name. The powerful name of Jesus! Greater is He that is in us, than he that is in the world (1 John 4:4).

This reminded me of another time years earlier when we were in the car. My husband was driving, I was in the passenger seat, and the kids in the back. Our youngest daughter was drinking from her sippy cup when all of the sudden, she made a weird sound. I looked and realized she was drowning. She could not catch her breath. She was literally turning purple. I took off my seatbelt and jumped in the back of the van and screamed that powerful name, "Jesus, Jesus!" She was back instantly. I encourage Christians to use that name. That's all that we have and it's all that we need. The name of Jesus is a powerful weapon that raises the dead, heals the sick, and sets captives free (Luke 4:18).

We were in a restaurant one day as a lady smiled at me. To me, that is an open door to start a quick conversation. She had a big tattoo of the image of Jesus on her back, so I asked, "Do you know him?" "Who?" She responded. I continued, "Him, the one in the picture on your back, Jesus Christ?" Right there she realized that she did not know him. She had that tattoo there just for religious reasons. I explained to her more about Him, what He did for her and who He is. I told her about His salvation and encouraged her to consider receiving Him as her Lord and Savior, then left her alone to enjoy her meal. I just planted the seed or maybe I watered the seed that was already planted in her heart. Nonetheless, I shared the gospel and allowed God to do the work. Go into all the earth and preach the gospel (Mark 16:15)!

I enjoy telling people about our miracles, but in this book, as I said before, I want to tell the whole world the things that happened before these miracles arrived. That's what gives others the courage to live a life that glorifies God despite the difficult times of patiently waiting. In this world, we will have trials and tribulations, but take heart He has overcome the world. He will never leave us or forsake us. This is what it means to be a Christian. We must believe without doubt that God's Word will come to pass in our lives. I believe God, regardless of my circumstances. I refuse to ignore the voice of the Holy Spirit in my heart. He taught me that believing Him is honoring Him (John 16:33; Deuteronomy 31:6).

For a while, we had our old van we brought from Ohio, and my stepfather blessed us with a very old Honda that he had. For us it was a blessing at the moment because we needed it, but later it became a terrible headache. This car would leave us stranded everywhere. It was one of those cars. I'm not kidding. I would park it, take the key out of the ignition, but the car engine would still be running for ten to twenty seconds until finally it would slowly stop on its own. At one point because of a terrible car-crash I had, we lost the van and ended up having this ugly car as our only family car—our only transportation.

There was no room for the whole family to ride together, so for us to go to church, we made two trips, or sometimes the church allowed Shawn to use one of the church's cars. I remember one specific time when I had to get out of the car and, with my oldest children, push the car in the middle of the road to make it work to bring us back home. It was embarrassing and tiresome. This specific time, I was holding back my tears. I didn't want my children to see my disappointment, so I stood on a corner and in silence, I prayed, "God, I am tired of living life like this. Look at my family. God, please change this, I trust in you." And at that moment, I knew that our situation was about to change (John 14:13).

I went home and talked to Shawn about going to look for a car, and he agreed. We drove our car to meet with a friend from church who worked as a car salesman. We were so sure that day we would go back home with our new car, and that the long struggle was going to end. We parked our ugly old Honda and walked inside. Our friend was so happy to see us and he quickly started the process. We gave him all our information and he went to speak to the sales manager to get our credit application approved. While we waited, through the glass dealership wall, we saw a couple walking in the car lot right in front of us. They were laughing and pointing at our ugly Honda. This couple was enjoying the mockery of comparing our car with the other customer cars parked up front. We actually thought it was funny to see them laughing at our car. Honestly, we laughed too. The car was an eye sore and barely ran when you needed it and would not stop running when the key was removed. It was time to say goodbye to that embarrassing headache. But when our friend came back, he did not look so happy. It was because he was about to tell us the news that he knew would break our hearts more than it broke his. He was not able to help us because of our financial situation. We were declined any credit because our income was too low. I remember looking at his lips when he said, "You guys don't qualify." God doesn't call the qualified–He qualifies the called (1 Corinthians 1:27–29).

Now we weren't laughing. We were embarrassed to drive out of that dealership in the same car that strangers made fun of, but we had no choice. There was complete silence as we drove back home. Not one of us could say anything. Once again, we were walking out of the line sad and frustrated. We could not break the silence of disappointment that consumed our hearts. We have been in situations like this one too many times in our lives. Remember when we had to walk out of the line in bible college and make room for those who were financially qualified? Or when we had to go home disappointed and throw our children's school tuition papers in the garbage because we did not qualify? I remember many times walking in places like the mall looking down hoping I would find some money to buy my children at least an ice cream cone. That's how financially broke we were. Do not take me wrong, God always provided, but that doesn't take away the fact that we went through all of this while waiting for our miracles to happen. That day on my mind, I kept thinking that we would never qualify for anything and I was tired of it. But I could not let my emotions take control. I wanted to encourage my husband, even though deep in my heart, I needed some encouragement myself. However, it wasn't just my husband and me that I was thinking about, but our children. I knew that they were excitedly waiting for us at home to come with our new car. Finally, Shawn and I broke the silence by laughing at the couple that was laughing at our car. That helped us to keep the joy and our trust in God. Laughter is like medicine to our bones. It is amazing how a little laughter in the middle of a circumstance like this one can change everything. It might not immediately change your situation, but it changes your attitude about the situation–and that is huge (Proverbs 17:22). It brought our faith back after a moment of discouragement and disappointment. We didn't know what we were going to tell our children or how this was going to happen, but we began to put our hope and trust in God. He knows it all, and yes, we have been in many situations like this one, but God! We knew that He was going to bring us through this one also (Ephesians 2:4).

We ended up borrowing my brother's car to use while he went to the Marines for a week or two. Then months later, we met a man at our church who just moved from Tennessee. My husband came home one day from work and he told me that something strange happened. He rarely answered the church phone, but that day at one specific time he did. It was this man looking for a church to attend with his family. They talked and when Shawn hung up the phone, he heard God saying, "Stay connected with that man, he'll help you one day." We both kept this in our hearts. Later on, we found out he works for a different dealership, and we decided to go try again to get our car, now that our finances were in better shape than months before. He was so happy to see us and to help us. He took our information and went to do the approval process. Minutes later, he came back to give us the news. He had no idea how intense this moment was for us. I began to speak in tongues inside my head. His long and fast steps felt so short and slow to me at the moment. Once again, we were hoping to go home with a new car, and we knew that our children were also once again desperate waiting at home. My heart was pounding, and finally he got to us and with a big smile on his face, he said, "We're good!" Awwwwww, thank you Lord. We went home with a Toyota Sienna. While we were leaving, that man took some cash out of his pocket and gave it to Shawn, saying; "Take your children out for dinner." I have to admit that right now, typing this story, tears are running down my cheeks, because I remember this moment. God is so faithful in all of His ways (Psalm 145:17; Deuteronomy 32:4).

In case you didn't know, there is always a story to tell before the miracle happens, and that's what I want people to know. I am a Christian woman who trusts God with all of my mind and heart, and in all of my ways, I acknowledge Him, and He makes my path straight (Proverbs 3:5–6).

We got home and there they were at the window waiting for us to come home in our new car. Yes, our four children. They were more excited than we were. They may never say it or show their frustration and embarrassment of us driving that ugly Honda, but I know they were. This meant a lot to them and I was happy for them to see that God has always been a promise keeper in our lives

(2 Corinthians 1:20). He always comes through, regardless of our situation. The Word says, "He will bless all the works of our hands" (Deuteronomy 28:12). So, let's put our hands to work!

Our children are now older and have witnessed the miracles of God in our lives all these years. Above all, they have seen us, their parents, worshiping our God with all of our hearts. Remember in the beginning of this book, I told my story of when I asked God to give me a husband. I was very specific with my request. I asked for a man who would put God's desires first. A man who would please God and not man. The reason for that request was because deep in my heart I wanted a godly family. I wanted to raise not just a family, but a "godly" family that would represent the glory of God. That was my greatest desire, so, whatever the cost, I was ready to follow God's instruction for this to happen (Proverbs 16:20). I strongly believe that whatever I ask in the name of Jesus, He will give it to me, and He has (John 14:13). I believe God (Matthew 21:22)!

Finally, after being basically homeless in a relative's basement, we were getting on our feet. We both were working hard. Shawn was working at the church and I started my own business cleaning houses on weekends, on top of the part-time job I had in the school. I was able to manage the whole thing, even my responsibilities at home, until one day when the school offered me some more work, more hours, more responsibilities, and more money. I was tired of never having enough so I took it. But see, everything needs a balance. It is easy for a blessing to become a burden if we are not careful. Now I was working full-time as a teacher in the school. Literally, I began to serve two masters (Matthew 6:24) Please, do not take me wrong. I'm talking about my own experience, my own heart. I took those extra hours at the school because of money, even though I knew that it was going to become a heavy weight on my shoulders. There was no need for me to do that. Having the part-time job and the cleaning business on weekends was enough–plus the responsibilities I had at home as a wife and a mother. My children needed me the most, they were very young at that time.

I started to feel frustrated. I had no time to seek first His kingdom and His righteousness. At this point, I was doing it in my own strength (Matthew 6:33).

If you are a full-time teacher, I bow my sombrero to you. I strongly encourage my children to always pray for their teachers, to pay attention in class, and overall to be extremely respectful and considerate of their teachers' hard work. Their job never ends; they bring it home on top of the pile of work they have at home. As a mother and wife, I was not able to do my job well. I began to walk away from those responsibilities. My job at the school was consuming me and I had to admit that I felt obligated to do it because I started to let my financial dependency be upon this, and not upon God, my provider.

It's easy for us to lose focus of our real call when we find a resource that covers our needs. The funny thing is that we somehow think that it is easier when it's not; it is actually harder on us when we are doing it in our own strength. The difference is in the natural, we can see it with our eyes–it is there. We think there is no need for faith. Working reassures me that I get a paycheck at the end of the week. This is what the Bible is talking about when it says, God will bless the work of our hands. The problem is when this becomes an idol and we take on more and more because of greed. Working too many jobs to make money became my focus because my family had a need. I could let go of the cleaning business or refuse to take the extra responsibility at the school, but instead I wanted it all, even though it was costing me my own family–which I thought I was doing all this for. We need to be careful in what our choices are and always remember that we cannot take God out of the picture. We have to always trust in Him, which should be the most important thing in our life (Luke 12:24).

At this point, what started as a blessing became a burden to me. I was not spending time with my husband. He would remove the laptop computer from my lap almost every night while I fell asleep preparing for my next day at work. My children were doing everything on their own, the house was a mess, and my time with the Lord was cut short. I was becoming a very tired, angry, and frustrated person. Every day while driving to the school, I cried tears of confusion and disappointment, asking God to help me. I was overwhelmed. One day, while seeing my children jump in the car ready for school, I was feeling so guilty to see that their uniforms weren't ironed, and their hair was messy. They looked like abandoned children, and in some ways, they were. I abandoned my obligation as a mother. I was too busy trying to help my husband pay our bills. Maybe the situation with our car and the words "You don't qualify" were so stuck in my heart that I did whatever I had to do to never hear that again (1 John 2:16).

A year later, I asked the school to take back the extra responsibility they had given me, but it was too late. They explained that they needed me full time at this point or not at all. I began to think on what to do then, my cleaning business was succeeding, and I was able to manage my own schedule. I was so confused (1 Corinthians 14:33).

One day, I stood in the parking lot of the school crying and I asked God to speak. "God, I won't move until you speak to me." It was there when I realized that I allowed my financial situation to overwhelm me. I unwisely took on more work than what I could do, and it was costing me everything I had–my joy, my peace, my marriage, my family, and, above all, my relationship with God. I walked into the principal's office with my intention to resign. I wanted it to happen right at that moment, that's how overwhelmed I was. She convinced me to rethink my decision and to, at least, finish the last three months of the school year, which I didn't do. Finally, the time came, and I was released from the pressure of that job. I remember calling my husband on the phone and the first thing he said was, "Yay, I have my wife back." Better a dry crust with peace and quiet than a house full of feasting with strife (Proverbs 17:1). The wisest of women builds her house, but folly with her own hands tears it down (Proverbs 14:1).

I want to be clear; I am not saying that all teachers should quit their jobs because it is hard. We must work hard. What I am saying is that the full-time job didn't work for me. Having all of these responsibilities not only stressed me out, but it gave me overwhelming pressure. Though I have to admit that I loved teaching students. That was one of the best experiences I had and I'm thankful for it. Let us keep in mind also that some things are just for a season. I knew that mine was over at the school (Proverbs 4:6–7).

We were still living in the same house that we rented when we first moved out of the basement. Our children loved that house. I hoped that maybe we could buy it one day. But who would think that one day we would be obligated to run out of that house and never come back? Yes, we were affected by Superstorm Sandy that hit the East Coast in October 2012. I remember that morning, we were so excited, thinking that we were going to have fun, watch some television, eat some food, and just see the storm pass by. A lot of areas were evacuated, but our neighborhood had a non-mandatory evacuation, so we decided to stay and enjoy ourselves (Isaiah 55:8–9).

The storm started and it was different than any other storm I saw in the United States. At 2 p.m., a big tree that was in front of our house was swinging around, almost kissing the ground with the top of its branches. That made me rethink our idea of staying in the house during this storm. I went to my room and got on my knees and I desperately asked God to speak to my heart. "God, what should we do? Should we stay here?" And from the inside, immediately, I heard, "Do whatever brings peace to you." Right there, I knew exactly what would bring peace to my heart, it was leaving the house immediately. While getting out of the room, Shawn came in and said to me, "There is water coming down the roof in the bathroom, I think we need to evacuate." We both agreed, grabbed a box full of personal documents, and left for a friend's house.

We had no time to grab anything else because at that point the storm was intensifying, so we left in our new Sienna van and left that old ugly Honda car in our garage. The next morning, we were surprised to hear about the damage that this storm produced. We tried to return to our home, but we couldn't. Our entire neighborhood was under at least four feet of water. We needed a boat to go around our neighborhood. We saw the paramedics helping people and their pets get out of their homes. Our next-door neighbor was asking for help on social media in the middle of the night. He needed someone to come rescue him, his wife, and their newborn baby, all trapped on the second floor of their home the night of the storm (Proverbs 16:9).

Finally, after two days, I went by myself to the house as the water had already receded. While driving around the neighborhood, it was devastating to see all of our neighbor's stuff out in front of their homes in large piles. I started to increase my faith and believe that this was not going to be our case. We really worked hard to get on our feet, and I was confident that our house would be the only one completely dry and safe. I got to the door and I could smell mold and some other different bad odors. I put the key in and began to turn the knob. The door was unlocked, but it would not open, something was blocking it. I pushed again and it finally opened. I could not believe it. All of our stuff, the things I worked so hard for, and that I almost lost my family for by working more hours than I should, were destroyed–dirty, smelly, and wet. One thing that really caught my attention was the object that was blocking the door. It was Shawn's bible college plaque that he was awarded as the top student. It was intact. There was no damage, it was completely safe. However, everything else was destroyed. You could see the mark on the walls where the flood water raised to four feet high. We also had water coming through our roof. I knew that everything was gone. Our beds, clothes, everything was soaking wet and smelled horrible, including my cleaning supplies and items for my business, which I was not able to do for different reasons at this point.

The Scriptures say, "Do not store up for yourselves treasures on earth, where moths and vermin destroy, and where thieves break in and steal. But store up for yourselves treasures in heaven, where moths and vermin do not destroy, and where thieves do not break in and steal. For where your treasure is, there your heart will be also" (Matthew 6:19–21). And let me add, "Where superstorms can come and wipe everything away."

Shawn went back to work at the church the day after the storm as they were leading relief efforts. I went to look for him to tell him the bad news. We were both devastated, but we knew that God was going to restore everything. We knew that He would do it again. But now I had to face my children and tell them that once again we had nothing. I got to our friend's house and I remember the words that came out of the mouth of the husband who passed away a couple of years later–words I will never forget. He said, "Glennys, whatever we have in our bank account is yours to use for whatever your family needs." During our walk with God, we have met the most amazing and godly people. It's an honor to call them our friends. I thanked them and walked upstairs to talk to my children. I started by encouraging them to trust that God would restore us again. They insisted on seeing the house, so I took them. While driving, we were praying, quoting Scriptures and worshiping God. I had not even parked yet, when my youngest son ran out of the car, crying, looking through the window and saying, "This is my house, Mommy, and I want to come back. Please, Mommy, let's go in." I grabbed him and explained that we could not enter. I did not know if it was safe for us to go in.

Finally, after seeing them so desperate to go in, I opened the door and let them in. Each of them ran to their rooms and started to look for their favorite toys. I can't forget, my youngest daughter opened the closet door looking for her collection of "Build A Bear" bears that she had been collecting since she was two years old. She experienced the creation of each of them at the store and specially named them one by one, and now she could not even touch them. She cried calling them by their names. This broke my heart, but I needed to be strong for them, so there was no time for tears. I encouraged her by saying that she would get them back one day, even when I knew that this was more emotional for her because, even if we replaced those bears, it was the experience that counted more in her heart. She hand-picked them one by one, stuffed them, put their little hearts inside of them, named them and brought them home as her little friends. This might not make sense for some people, but for a child, this was her world. It was so sad to see my children, each of them looking at their favorite things and not being able to touch any of them. But God's grace is sufficient (2 Corinthians 12:9)!

We lost everything. Like all of our neighbors, we also had a pile of all of our belongings in front of our house for the town to pick up. This was so tragic. We received all of these things in an amazing way and now they were taken away from us. We went to the house another day to make sure everything was out and were about to leave when my youngest son began to call on his "Chickie." Oh no. I totally forgot about Chickie! This was his favorite stuffed animal. It was a small yellow chick in the form of a pillow that he slept with and carried everywhere, but the night of the storm, because of our rush to get out of the house, we forgot to take Chickie with us. So, we began to look for Chickie, but could not find it anywhere around the house. Finally, we decided to leave. Our hearts were broken. We got in our van and there was this silence. I began to drive and for some reason I decided to go back a different way than we came in. When all of a sudden, I heard my daughter scream, "Chickie, there is Chickie, Mommy." I stopped and got out of the car. I couldn't believe it. It was Chickie, all dirty and stinky, and maybe run over by hundreds of cars, but we still could recognize it. That was our Chickie! But my son had to let go because it was not safe to bring it home with us. These are some of the things that we as a family had to go through to get to our destiny. We learned to endure and persevere together in our faith. Sometimes let go and let God, even when things don't make sense, or they look tough. We always keep in mind that God's plan is better than ours (Exodus 14:14; Psalm 34:17; 2 Chronicles 15:7).

Our youngest son had also been collecting Hot Wheels cars since he was two years old. He had about five hundred of these cars collected in boxes. I totally forgot about them. What's so amazing is that he, by the grace of God, forgot or did not want to ask about it. I had my mind focused more on where we were going to live and what we should do. Early the next morning, I got a phone call from a very good and kind friend of mine, who also had a child who was my son's classmate. She said, "We found out that your family lost everything. The children at the school collected a whole bunch of Hot Wheel cars for David. Will it be OK if I bring them to him?" It was right there at that moment that I remembered my son's car collection. That was a sign from God to me, to remind me that we are not forgotten, and that God cares for everything, big or little. When I told my son about his friends collecting these cars for him, that made his day. He was so happy! He went through a lot because of all of this, but God! Those who hope in the LORD will renew their strength. They will soar on wings like eagles; they will run and not grow weary; they will walk and not be faint (Isaiah 40:31). Instead of your shame you will receive a double portion, and instead of disgrace you will rejoice in your inheritance. And so, you will inherit a double portion in your land, and everlasting joy will be yours (Isaiah 61:7).

During this time, we lost so many things that we did not even remember them until years later, maybe because of the way everything happened; it was so unexpected. Because of this storm, I lost my wedding dress, and I didn't even realize it until years later when a young lady wanted to get married. She needed a dress and I thought of letting her borrow mine, and at that moment I realized that it was gone. We lost a lot of material stuff, but not our good memories and our faith–that still remains (Hebrews 11:1; Psalm 46:10).

How ironic that now, once again, all that we had was our van, and that's where we spent most of the time. We wanted to give the family that we were staying with a break. We were a family of six and we know how difficult that can be. This family was a large family themselves, so we were trying to keep the load as light as possible. I called a friend and asked her if we could stay with them and they said, "Yes, but for one night only." We were sleeping in their basement, all of us together, our children on the couches and my husband and me on the floor. Yes, once again in a basement and on the floor, but at least this was a nice, finished basement.

In the middle of the night, I woke up hearing, "Do you trust me?" I really thought it was my friend's husband asking her that question, so I tried to cover my ears, thinking that I have no business listening to their conversation. I went back to sleep and once again I heard, "Do you trust me?" I woke up realizing that it was the voice of God. It was Him talking to my heart, and without hesitation, I responded, "Yes, Lord, I trust you." And He said, "Seek first my kingdom." And right there, with tears on my eyes, I asked, "What's your kingdom for me to follow right now? Lord, please tell me, what's your kingdom for me to follow?" Crystal clear, I heard, "Go back to the ministry." I knew exactly what He meant, go back to *Move the Earth*. But how? It did not make sense at that moment. Once again, we were homeless and getting all the help we could get from different churches and organizations, sleeping in friends' houses, and sometimes early in the morning we were going to Burger King's bathroom to brush our teeth. We had nothing, except one thing—our faith (2 Corinthians 5:7)!

Look at God's plan. Seriously look. Nothing, absolutely nothing can stop Him. It was about a week after the storm, when my phone kept ringing, but I didn't recognize the number, so I didn't answer. Finally, a friend from church called me and said, "Glennys, there's someone from our church trying to reach you. Please answer the phone." The next time it rang I immediately answered. Remember the man in the dealership who helped us buy our van and blessed us with some money to take our children out for dinner? The one that called the church from Tennessee looking for a home church to attend with his family as he relocated to New Jersey. The one that God told Shawn to stay connected to because he would help us one day? We thought that help was complete with the approval of a loan to purchase our van, but God had other plans. It was his wife calling me. She invited us to her house for dinner and we accepted. We came and they were the most pleasant people to be around. They lived in an amazing, beautiful, big house. At the dinner table, the man began to say something that shocked me. He said, "Shawn, remember the day I called the church for the first time, looking for a church to attend with my family and you answered?" "Yes!" responded Shawn. The man continued, "After that phone call, the Lord told me to stay connected to you and that I was going to help you one day." He started to cry and said, "Today is that day, we want to offer you and your family to live here with us for as long as you need, and you don't have to pay us anything." (1 Corinthians 1:9).

I knew in my heart that this was of God and that we were to say, "yes," but out of respect for my husband, I allowed him to make that decision. We were in our van and we talked about it with our children, and Shawn decided this offer was coming from God. A day or two later, we moved in with this amazing family. The first thing I did was look for a place where I could go every morning to hide myself in the presence of God. I could not do it in the living room because I would disturb this family's morning. I could not do it in the room that we were sleeping in because the noise would wake up my husband. I desperately looked for a place where I could be alone with God. I had no other option, then, but to do it in the closet. I brought a lamp with me, closed the door as much as possible, and sat on top of our shoes. This became my secret place. I honestly can say that without this morning encounter with my King, I could never have made it. Whose instruction would I follow? Knowing that He abides in me and I abide in Him, everything will work out for our lives in His sovereign plan. I cannot afford to depend on my own strength, but His (Psalm 27:1).

I experienced the Lord in many different and deep ways living in that house. He was my Teacher–my Master. On one occasion, I woke up and made a big breakfast for everybody. As I served my family, I was waiting for my friend, the lady of the house, to come downstairs. Her husband came down first, so to be nice and show my appreciation of this family's hospitality, I grabbed a plate and was about to serve him. Then I heard in my spirit, "What are you doing? That is not your place. It is his wife who serves him–not you." I put everything back and went to sit with my family. Only the spirit can hear the voice of the Spirit. It is important for us to understand and respect our place of position with others. We love and honor one another by respecting each other. I honestly can say that this type of wisdom and understanding only comes when we make God the master of our lives. He is our teacher, and He is alive in us. I have said this throughout this book, and I must restate it again–God is real. We have to learn to live by the Scriptures, not however we want. If we live by the Spirit, let us also walk by the Spirit (Galatians 5:25).

We had the best holiday season with this family. They made sure we were taken care of, especially our children. It was amazing how God put us together and became one family. We are forever thankful for them and with God for guiding our steps in the perfect path (Psalm 16:11)!

One day, close to Valentine's Day, I woke up from a dream. In my dream, I saw an ugly figure and was instructed by God to get closer. The figure looked as if it was having trouble breathing. I followed God's instruction and without fear I walked one step closer to the enemy's face. He was about to vomit while I was looking at him. Suddenly, he began to throw up all over me, but what he was throwing up were pounds of jewels and diamonds. There were so many attached to each other that I could hold them with both of my arms, and I heard God say, "He will pay back what he has stolen" (Proverbs 6:31).

I woke up so ecstatic about this. I was ready for a "Payback Time". I shared the dream with my husband, the lady that we lived with, and with some other ladies from my church. I was so excited, expecting to see what God was about to do. I kept thanking God for a payback time. I was confident it was about to happen because I believe God (1 Timothy 4:10)!

Early in the morning on Valentine's Day, the lady that we lived with and I were getting our children ready for school. We were in the kitchen, preparing their lunches, when we heard my youngest daughter, coming down the stairs screaming, "Mommy, mommy, Happy Valentine's day!" She handed me a card that she got days before when Shawn took her and her sister to Barnes and Nobles. No one knew what she bought, not even Shawn. She insisted I open the card she got me. I looked at my friend as we both smiled at my daughter's interruption and persistence for me to open that card. I opened it expecting a sweet, cute Valentine's Day message. Oh my goodness! I still have that card. In the front it says, "Mom, for all the LOVE you've given me over the years..." And inside it said, "Payback Time!" Remember, I never shared my dream with my children yet. This totally confirmed that God was speaking loud and clear (2 Samuel 22:14).

My friend and I looked at each other and literally screamed, "Nooooooo!" We could not believe it. We were in shock. If God was not speaking clearly to my heart, then what? I went around telling everybody about my dream and the card my daughter gave me. Yes, now I understand poor Joseph in the Bible when he did the same. It is extremely exciting hearing God and all I wanted was to tell everyone I know what was happening, because somehow, I knew deep in my heart that God was about to do it again–and He did (Jeremiah 1:12).

Four months went by as we looked for a house to rent. This was more difficult than normal because a lot of properties in the area were damaged from the superstorm. Since the market had many renters in need but few houses available, the rental owners were taking advantage of the situation by increasing the monthly amount above the regular value. Therefore, we could not afford much because we only had Shawn's income. Thankfully we got in a contract with a house. We were so anxious to hear from the realtor so we could move in. Finally, she called us to say, "I'm sorry, the owner decided to rent it to another family." Once again, we did not qualify. This started to get very frustrating for us. We were a family of six living in this gracious family's house for nearly five months. Though this family was very patient and kind to us, we wanted to have our own place. We continued to endure and be patient as we kept looking around and asking people about possible rentals (2 Peter 3:9).

I remember a specific day that I will never forget. It was a normal day, nothing out of the ordinary. I was at the house by myself and suddenly I felt God's presence. I could tell you that it was one of those visitations of the Lord. I prepared myself to take His instructions and He said, "The time will come where you will need to help Shawn carry the financial burden. Will you do that?" And I answered, "Yes." I honestly felt it was like when the angel came to Mary and told her, "You will have a son." I'm not kidding. This was so clear to me. He came to tell me that I needed to find a job. I know what you are thinking right now, "Did you really need God to tell you that? Was it not obvious that you needed to do that?" But you have to understand that many women like me (at that time) become comfortable not working. If the husband suggests that we need to find a source of income, it becomes a huge problem. We do not want to hear it. Believe me, God was helping by intervening in this spiritual moment of my life. After all, He is my Father, He knows me better than I know my own self. I personally have no explanation for this, but I'm sure that a lot of women need God to tell them too. Again, maybe I did not need to work full-time, as the pressure of work and family overwhelmed me before, but I had to do something. Could I work a couple of hours while the kids were at school, then take care of my responsibilities at home? Also, being at home 24/7 was not helpful for my mind, as I spoke about in an earlier chapter of this book. This was a big issue for me. A slack hand causes poverty, but the hand of the diligent makes rich (Proverbs 10:4). I began to open my eyes and look for something. I knew in my heart that God must already have this door open for me (Proverbs 13:4).

On another day, a friend of mine called me early in the morning and said, "Glennys, as you know I'm selling my house and moving to Florida, but this morning while praying, God spoke to me. I want to talk to you about it, can you please come to my house right now?" I was at her house within an hour. She said, "Go around my house and look at my furniture. I want you to tell me what you like." I did not fully understand what she was planning to do, but I did what she asked me to. The funny thing is she walked behind me and every piece of furniture that I touched she would tell me the cost of what she paid for. We came downstairs and she said, "The owner of the house I'm buying in Florida called me to say that I can keep all his furniture. We are not taking anything with us. Glennys, if you have $3,000 dollars all this furniture is yours. That's the amount we need to move." I could not believe it. I grabbed her hand and prayed, "Father, thank you, you are faithful, and you do not do half-miracles. Thank you for sending somebody with the $3,000 dollars that I need for this furniture. I give you the glory and the honor, Amen!" I told her, it will come from either your side or my side, but it will come, and I left. Now faith is the assurance of things hoped for, the evidence of things not seen (Hebrews 11:1).

Three days later, I was driving back home from dropping my husband at work when he called me, "Where are you? Turn around, come back." I came back and he said that a lady that we met years ago and who did not have any idea about our furniture situation came and gave him an envelope and said, "God told me to give this to you and your family." I opened it and it was a note saying, "For your furniture," with $3,000 dollars in it. I ran to my friend's house and asked her to open the envelope and to be a witness of the faithfulness of God. She was crying and rejoicing with me. At that moment, she realized her husband, who was not a believer yet and had a hard time believing in God, was minutes away from home. We decided to tell him this story to be a witness of how real God is (Ephesians 3:20).

We still had not found a house to rent, but we had most of our furniture. Yet, once again, God showed me that He is my provider and therefore I do not need to worry about my life–what I will eat or drink; or about my body, what I will wear. Is not life more than food, and the body more than clothes? Look at the birds of the air; they do not sow or reap or store away in barns, and yet my heavenly Father feeds them. Are we not more valuable than they? Can any one of us by worrying add a single hour to our lives (Matthew 6:25–27)?

At this same time, Shawn began to feel that it was time to go back to the ministry. One morning, very early, I was driving him to work, as we had to share the car. I noticed that something was troubling him. I asked what was happening. He shared with me his burden. He said, "God is asking me to go back to our ministry. I know it's time, but how? How can we do this?" We both knew that he would have to leave his job at the church to work full time in the ministry as he was not allowed to do both at the same time. We already experienced before what it is to do this, to obey God–and it was not easy. Honestly, many times I was tempted to say, forget the whole thing and let's just be a church attendee. That means working regular jobs or starting our own business and attending church on Sundays (2 Timothy 1:9).

Remember that our call is not to be pastors of a church. Financially, that would make it easier to plan our budget and manage our lives. A dedicated fraction of the people give their tithes. However, they do feel connected and give on a regular, consistent basis. But as a para-church ministry, we have to look for ministry partners and raise our own financial support through the mail. The people who are more apt to give must first give their tithe to their local church. Then if there is any discretionary money left over, they can give us and other ministries a smaller amount. To imagine Shawn was going to leave his job to do the ministry full-time again was not an easy thing to agree to–but it was necessary. That was the only way we could move on with what we were compelled in our hearts to do–to move the earth.

We both knew that God was asking us to continue with the call. We had no doubt about it. It was at that moment that we both decided to obey God regardless of our situation and say, "Yes," to our call to go back and continue our ministry. I dropped Shawn at the church, and he resigned.

Within minutes of our decision, I received a phone call (1 Samuel 15:22). It was the same lady who gave us the money for our furniture. She said, "Glennys, do you and Shawn have a ministry?" I replied, "What? Why?" I was so confused. And she repeated, "Do you and Shawn have a ministry?" I could not help but think of the decision we just made minutes before saying "yes" to God to relaunch *Move the Earth.* I responded, "Yes." She said, "I was praying, and God told me that I need to plant the first seed for your ministry." She gave us $7,000 dollars! That precious and timely gift, made possible by her obedience to God, helped us to relaunch the ministry here in the state of New Jersey. We know God will credit her account in Heaven for the impact the ministry has had over the years.

Shawn became the face of *Move the Earth*–reversing the trend of biblical unbelief. The steps of a [good and righteous] man are directed and established by the Lord. And He delights in his way [and blesses his path] (Psalm 37:23).

Review–Even though God proved many times that He is my provider, instead of patiently waiting in faith, I went and attempted things in my own strength. This repeatedly made my situation worse. Physically and mentally, it brought overwhelming stress–and for what? At the end, in one blink of an eye, everything was gone.

Encouragement–Be a hard worker, not a greedy worker. Always put God first. Do what brings peace to your heart and the heart of your loved ones. Use wisdom from God. Maintain patience in your endurance. Trust and believe God regardless of the circumstances.

Apply–James 3:13, 17; Proverbs 1:7; 3:5–8; 4:6–7; 11:2; 13:10; 14:1; 16:16; 19:20; Ephesians 5:15–16; Psalm 23:1; 56:3–4; 1 John 2:15; 4:18; Isaiah 26:3–4; Hebrews 11:6; Matthew 6:19, 24; 7:11, 31–33; Philippians 4:19.

Learned–I learned that I have to build my house, not destroy it. In order to do that, I have to walk by the Spirit. I had to rethink my priorities and not allow doubt and unbelief to cause me to worry about how we would make ends meet. What you might consider a blessing might become a burden if you attempt to do things in your own strength.

Chapter 7

My Greater "Payback Time" Experience!

Five months went by and we were still living with that family. We are forever thankful for them. With all humility and gentleness, with patience, we bear with one another in love (Ephesians 4:2). Shawn was working his final two weeks at the church. We were getting very frustrated about not finding a house to rent as we both knew that it was time for us to live in our own place with our own family.

Finally, it happened! I was in a doctor's office when a lady I know asked me if I found a house yet, as many people were aware of how desperately we were looking. She handed me a phone number and said, "Call my Mom and ask her to rent you her house. I know she is selling it, but she may consider renting it to you." I didn't even wait to go home or talk to Shawn; right from my car I called and she answered. I explained to her our situation and she asked me to come to see the house. We went that same day and were ready to sign the rental contract. They took all of our information and told us that they would call us to let us know their decision. We prayed and patiently waited for their call (Romans 12:12).

Three days later, they called to say that they decided to rent it to us. We were so excited to move in right away. We had enough to pay our security deposit and a month's worth of rent. We already had most of our furniture, which we went to pick up from my friend's house, who later moved to Florida. We had so much fun in that house. We had many family members and friends over and hosted launch meetings in our basement for our ministry, *Move the Earth*.

I realized that we needed some lamps and lamp tables for our living room because it was too dark in that area of the house. I asked God to provide it for us. You won't believe this story. I went to look for them at a thrift store and found that they had these beautiful lamps there. I wanted them so badly, but we did not have the money to buy them. They also had the perfect lamp tables for my house. They were very expensive because they were made of fancy marble. I told the manager, who I knew very well, how in love I was with those specific items. She gave me their prices but obviously I could not afford them. However, I promised her that I was going to come back to get them. While sitting in my van in the thrift store parking lot, I told God how I wanted those things and He said, "They're yours!" I got so excited and I started to thank Him because I believed Him. I presented my request to God and His peace assured me that it was done, as He has done many times in my life before (Philippians 4:6–7).

I was still volunteering in the children's ministry of our church. During a Wednesday night service, I was helping with a sweet lady. Shawn could not make it to church that day, so he dropped me off and I told him that I was going to find a ride to get back home. I asked the lady that I was volunteering with if she could take me home and she said, "Yes." The time came for us to go back home and when I was getting into her car, to my surprise, she had the exact two lamps I saw in the thrift store in her car. Immediately I asked her, "You bought them?" No, she said and asked me, "Do you like them?" "I love them," I responded and she said, "Then they're yours." "What? Where did you get them from?" I asked. She responded, "On my way here, I noticed my neighbor threw them away, so I picked them up and brought them in my car just in case, but I don't even know if they work." I couldn't believe it. I went home with my beautiful lamps and they worked perfectly (Philippians 4:19).

Now we had the lamps, but they sat on the floor because we did not have lamp tables yet. I stopped by the store many times just to look at them and make sure no one bought them. I knew that they were mine, so I kept patiently waiting. After three weeks, I got a phone call from an organization asking me to call back and I did. A man answered, and said, "Mrs. Hyland, I'm calling on behalf of an organization, FEMA gave us your number. Do you know a thrift store called...?" "Yes," I answered as I realized he was asking for the same thrift store where the lamp tables were. He continued, "I left there a voucher with your name and the amount of money we are granting you. Go and ask the manager for it." It was the exact amount for both tables! Who other than God can do that? I drove to the store immediately. I was dancing as I watched the workers put my tables into my van. Finally, my lamp tables were home. The Lord is my shepherd; I shall not want (Psalm 23:1).

Remember the ugly Honda car we had? The car insurance could not give us anything for it, not because of the condition of the car, but because when the superstorm hit, we left it inside the garage and it was damaged by water. The insurance explained that if the car was in the driveway and a tree would have fallen on top of it, then they would pay the value of the car, but unfortunately that was not the case. Even though that big tree that was in front of our house swinging around, almost kissing the ground with the top of his branches did fall on our driveway in the exact spot where the car was normally parked, the car was not there. According to their rules and regulations, they were not obligated to cover it. But another well-known organization that is there to help natural disaster victims, called and asked for the list of everything we lost. The lady questioned us about that same car. I personally was not too interested in answering her questions about that car, because for me that car had no value, so I tried to dismiss the conversation. She stopped me and said, "Ma'am, it doesn't matter the condition of the car. Whatever the car looked like, it was your transportation and that's what counts." They gave us a substantial amount of money to replace that ugly car. Yes, the one that strangers made fun of when we turned away. Yes, the one that when you took the keys out, it was still running. I could not believe it. The devil paid it back (Proverbs 6:31).

God never stops working His miracles. He wants to use us, but we have to be willing. He is always speaking and giving instructions to His people, to those who do not harden their hearts and obey His voice. "My sheep listen to my voice; I know them, and they follow me" (John 10:27).

There was another Wednesday, as we were going to church, right at the door of my house, I heard, "Take one of your Bath and Body hand soaps with you." I paused everything, told my family to wait, though they were already in the car. I asked God, "A hand soap?" He said, "Yes, a hand soap." I obeyed whatever He asked me to do, so I went back inside, grabbed a hand soap and put it in my purse. I got to church and did not think about the soap. Honestly, I totally forgot about it, but not God, He did not forget. After the service was finished, everyone was leaving and I was ready to go home too, but I heard Him saying to me, "In the right side of the building, there's a woman still sitting down, bring her the soap and tell her that I want her to know that I care for her." I looked up and yes, there she was. I walked towards the lady and I said exactly what God told me to tell her and gave her the soap. She started to cry. She could not talk–but cried. Her husband, who is an usher, looked at us and came closer to her. When he saw the soap, he was astonished and asked, "Did she just give you that soap?" She said, "Yes, she did." And they both were going crazy. Then she explained to me that they lived with her mother-in-law, and right before she was leaving to go to church, she used the bathroom. There was no hand soap for her to wash her hands with and because she told her mother-in-law about it, they had an argument. That upset her very badly, and here I was with a hand soap from God to give her and telling her that He cares for her! Guide my steps, God, and let my ears hear your voice and your voice only to follow (Psalm 119:133–135).

Let me say that being obedient to God this way is not easy. Even though I am used to doing it, it is still not easy. I still get nervous and my mind goes crazy telling me things like, "What if it's not God speaking to you? Or what if they laugh at you? Or what if this or that?" But, according to my experiences, it always works. I am God's sheep and I hear and recognize His voice. I know when He is speaking to my heart. I do not go around doing things in my own way looking for things to happen. That is not how this works. I listen and obey the voice of my Shepherd. When He speaks, no matter what He asks me to do, I do it. Even when it does not make sense, like in this case, He asked me to bring a "hand soap," and a hand soap I brought. The rest is up to Him. He is REAL!

Another Wednesday at church, after service, I was leaving when the Holy Spirit directed my eyes towards a lady that was standing all the way in the back and He said to me, "Go and speak life in her life." I noticed that almost everyone was gone and she was not moving. She was just standing with her head down, so I went over to her and I hugged her. I began to speak the Word over her life, "You're strong and not weak (2 Corinthians 12:10). He has plans to prosper you and not to harm you, plans to give you hope and a future (Jeremiah 29:11). The thief comes only to steal and kill and destroy. Jesus came that you may have life and have it abundantly (John 10:10). With long life he will satisfy you (Psalm 91:16). He is your strong tower (Proverbs 18:10). He is your refuge and your strength (Psalm 46:1). He will never leave you, nor forsake you (Hebrews 13:5)."

She started to cry. At first, she tried to push me away, but I hugged her tight and did not let go, until I felt the peace of God guarding her mind. She hugged me back and said nothing, but I knew at

that moment she was free from whatever was oppressing her.
Then I said goodbye and we went home. For the Word of God
is living and active, sharper than any two-edged sword, piercing
to the division of soul and of spirit, of joints and of marrow, and
discerning the thoughts and intentions of the heart (Hebrews 4:12).

Months later, I was walking with my family, coming out of church
in the parking lot, when I heard a woman behind me, "Excuse
me, excuse me." I stopped and a lady came over to me and asked,
"Remember me? I am the lady that one day you went at the end
of a service in the back of the church and hugged me." "Oh yes,"
I responded, and she continued "That day (tears started to run
down her face), I wanted to end my life and you came and spoke
the Word over me, and peace came to my heart. Thank you!" She
hugged me. I honestly did not know what to respond to her, other
than encourage her to go and do the same for other women that
might be in the same situation she was. God is faithful. Let us use
the discernment that He gave us for His purpose!

What amazes me is how God orchestrates everything in such
a perfect way that at times our natural mind cannot even
comprehend it. At the end of that year, this same lady who stopped
me in the parking lot blessed my family in an unexpected way.
Who would think of this? God's plans are just incredible. That
particular December, we wanted to surprise our children and give
them as a Christmas present, a trip to Disney World. Our oldest
child was getting so big and we could never afford to take them
there, or on any vacation. We knew many families who went
multiple times, but we never had the opportunity to go once.
However, Shawn and I felt in our hearts that it was time for us to
believe God for this trip, especially after the storm wiped us out
a year earlier. We have always believed for many other things while
serving in the ministry–why not this (Matthew 6:33).

We went to a travel agency and walked out discouraged, thinking
that maybe we were just dreaming. They wanted a lot of money for

a package for six people. So, we continued to pray for this and ask God for His direction. Let me remind you that it was something that no one knew, just my husband and me. We wanted to surprise our children with this and we also wanted to be debt free.

One day, out of the blue, this lady called me and said, "I was praying and God told me to ask you what you want to give your children this Christmas." So, not expecting anything from her, other than her prayers of agreement, I told her our biggest desire: surprise our children with a trip to Disney World, and to my surprise—what a perfect God we serve—she said, "I can help you with that. I will give you the passes to the parks." Say what? I almost fell out of my chair. She blessed us with the park passes and days later, someone else gave us a check with the exact amount for the flights and the hotel. This person did not have any idea of our plan. He came to us and blessed us with that check saying, "This is for your children's Christmas gift." At the end, we just ended up paying for the food. We give God the glory in all of this. Whatever we ask in His name, He will give it to us (John 14:13). That is how faithful God is with those who patiently wait and trust in Him.

I remember that Christmas morning, our four children opened their small gift and then I took out a big present for all of them to unwrap together. They looked at me and thought it was a joke. They unwrapped it really fast and I screamed, "A luggage." I asked them to open it. I could not wait to see their reaction. They sort of slowed down as they unwrapped it, probably still thinking it was a joke. One of them unzipped the luggage and that was when they saw a Mickey Mouse stuffed animal holding the tickets and the travel guide with our whole plan to visit Disney World. They screamed so loud! The big smiles on their faces will stay in my heart forever. The joy in their hearts was so evident. Our oldest literally passed out. What a moment and what a financial release that was. God, you did it! You are amazing and great is your faithfulness (Lamentations 3:22–23)!

That Christmas will forever remain unforgettable. We had so many blessings coming in. Even Home Depot surprised us with presents for our four children and a real Christmas tree. This was our first "real" tree. We also had a lady that I met at one of the schools that I worked at bring gifts and Christmas dinner to our family. God is so good. We went on our Disney World vacation in January and it was the most amazing time together as a family. To see our children so excited and enjoying everything was priceless. They went through a lot that year and all of this was "Payback Time" for us. And my God will meet all your needs according to the riches of His glory in Christ Jesus. To our God and Father be the glory for ever and ever. Amen (Philippians 4:19–20).

A new year came and it was time for our children's annual checkups. To my surprise, the doctor told me that she could hear an abnormality in one of our child's hearts and that I needed to take him to a cardiologist. We made the appointment and they did a lot of tests. While waiting for the results, we prayed and confessed the Word over his life. I stood firm and told the devil that we were not going to accept his lie and we were not going to play his game. "Put it back devil. Put back our son's health. We submit to the spirit of God; we resist you and you must flee from us." (James 4:7). I know that God gave us power to overcome all the work of the enemy, and sickness and disease is an oppression of the devil, so together, we resisted it as a family. We went to see the cardiologist and he gave us the good news. It was nothing serious, just a little bit of stress and that we needed to cut out caffeinated drinks. Our son's heart was back to normal. Thank you, Jesus!

It was at this time of my life that I started not just looking for any job, but believing for a good job. I started praying and fasting for ten days, asking God to direct my steps, as He promised. I was in my third day of fasting, and once again, I was volunteering in the children's ministry of my church. As I was taking care of babies in the nursery room, a friend was passing by the classroom door, and I said, "Hey, keep me in prayer, I'm believing for a job." She walked back and literally started to cry. "What happened?" I asked. Looking at my eyes, she said, "Glennys, my husband's assistant just quit and while driving here I asked God to help us to find that one person to take this position. That person is you. You start this Friday at 8 a.m." For a moment I had no words ... wait, I have no experience as a dental assistant. "How is this going to work?" I asked. "I'll train you," she responded, and continued walking into the sanctuary. And just like that, I had a new job. New position. New profession. I am still working there many years later. I do everything in that office, including X-rays. Years later, I went to a technical school and earned my radiology license. God is blessing the work of my hands (Isaiah 41:10; 2 Corinthians 9:10).

I have no doubt that it is God who opened wide this door in my life for a different reason than just to pay my bills. This time I was seeing things differently; something had changed. I know that I am to be diligent and represent Him in everything I do and to work hard. That If anyone forces me to go one mile, I need to go with them two miles (Matthew 5:41). I have done just what He asked me to. I learned to do everything, not to receive rewards from men, but because God's eyes are upon me and He sees it all, and His rewards are eternal. If I ever had a desire to be a missionary, this right here became the moment. It is as if I have been sent to do what a missionary does, minister to strangers until God says, "Mission accomplished." Let me clarify, I was sent there to work as a dentist assistant and that has been my priority from day one, but at the same time, I have been given the opportunity to do the work of God in a way that only He could orchestrate.

My eyes have seen more people than ever giving their life to Jesus. People have received healing in their bodies, restoration of broken hearts, and families have come together because of the power of Jesus Christ (Matthew 10:8). I have prayed for a lot of people who are fighting depression and anxiety. By the grace of God, they opened up to me, and as a Christian, I give them what I have—Jesus Christ. Many have received Him as their Lord and Savior (1 Peter 5:7).

I have prayed for people who have been on drugs for years and they were set free. Single mothers, who were not able to raise their own children because of addiction or depression, received the salvation of Jesus Christ, and suddenly became responsible and involved parents again. Other parents who could not sleep because they were concerned about their children who were addicted to drugs, alcohol, and other substances. Grandparents who are concerned for their grandchildren. Marriages that were falling apart.

This world is full of hurting people who desperately need the salvation of our Lord Jesus Christ (Psalm 124:7–8).

A grandmother shared with me her concerns about Thanksgiving dinner with her family. She said, "My whole family comes to my house and I hate it." "Why?" I asked. Her answer shocked me. She said, "Because I can't get along with any of them. We all hate each other and all that we do is fight and fight." I looked at her in her eyes and said, "That could change this year if you want it to." She asked, "How? It's always the same and I wish I could just tell them not to come anymore." I responded, "No, that's not the solution. You want them to come, they're your family." And I began to tell her about the forgiveness of Jesus Christ. I explained to her that she was hurt and hurting others, and that she needed to receive forgiveness in her heart. She was crying and humbled herself before God, confessed her sins, and received Jesus as her Lord and Savior. She went home happy with a different expectancy for her Thanksgiving dinner with her family (Ephesians 4:32; 1 John 1:9; Matthew 6:14–15)! Forgiveness has a greater effect when we recognize that we also have hurt others and need them to forgive us. I have to forgive, as God has forgiven me. My heart was healed when I admitted that I hurt others and needed their forgiveness, then it became easy for me to let go of those who hurt me. Admitting my own wrongdoing helps me to give grace to those who do wrong.

Another lady walked toward me and asked, "Can I pinch you? I want to see if you are real. Why are you always so happy? You have no problems?" My answer changed her life that day. "Yes, Ma'am, I have problems and situations just like you, but I also have a savior who carried them all. His name is Jesus. I bring everything to His feet and exchange my yoke for His." I was not even done when she started to cry and received Jesus as her Lord and Savior. Let me stop right here and say that there are people in the world who cannot stand those who carry the joy of the Lord. We live in a world where society is being trained to walk angry, sad, or depressed. For them this is normal, but when they see someone full of joy, they think that there is a problem. In other words, the world thinks that walking sad, angry, and depressed is normal, but happiness, joy, and an abundant life are not normal. It is so foreign to these people. They believe that those who have peace have a mental health issue or are in denial of something. Therefore, they see you as if something is wrong with you. At least, this has been my experience. People not only at my place of work, but in the stores or in restaurants have asked me the same question. "Why are you so happy?" The funny thing is the look on their faces (Matthew 11:30).

Joy does not just automatically come to us. We have to choose it, regardless of our position in life. We have to believe in our hearts that God is bigger than our problems and situations. The Bible says that the joy of the Lord is our strength, so if we allow the enemy to take our joy, then he takes our strength and with that goes everything, including our vision. How do I fight without strength? This is my little secret. Like Samson, he had a secret of where his strength came from but he gave it away. Do not allow your enemy to cut your joy the way Samson's enemy cut his hair and poked his eyes out (Nehemiah 8:10).

One time in a restaurant, I was signing my bill, but the pen the cashier gave me to use did not work. It happened to the customer right before me and he gave her a big deal because of it. But I told her not to worry, I was going to use my own. While leaving, I gave my pen to her to keep. She, with a very serious look on her face, asked me, 'Why are you giving me your pen and why are you so happy?" She acted as if she was offended, not because I was giving her a pen, but because I was showing her love and compassion. People in this world are not used to kindness, respect, and love. This is tragic. God is love and He lives in me and it is by loving others that I spread Him to the world around me. We are not called to become or act like the world, but to be different (Romans 12:2).

I met a precious lady battling cancer. We had many conversations about the Lord. She received Him as her Lord and Savior, and since that day, something changed within her. She even told me that the fear was gone and that she had peace and felt this inexplicable joy in her heart. Unfortunately, she passed away, but what amazed me was, her children came to me and said, "Thank you, for what you did to our mom. She died with so much peace and joy, and she told us about Jesus." I cannot stress enough how faithful God is (2 Timothy 2:13).

While God was using me with others, I had my own situations to deal with, but Matthew 6:33 says that if I seek first His kingdom and His righteousness, all these things will be added unto me. At this time in our lives, we were having some situations with the house we were renting and we were obligated to find another house to rent. Because the owner of this house was not coming through with their obligations as a landlord. Each time there was a heavy rain, water came inside the basement up to four inches. The landlord did not take care of it, it eventually produced mold. We took care of it many times because of our health, until we got tired of the owners not taking responsibility. We were a month ahead in our rent at that time and took good care of that property as if it was our own, yet every year they gave us a new contract with the rent raised a significantly higher amount. We were working hard and felt extremely tight financially because of the amount of money that we were paying in rent. It was just not right that landlords were taking advantage of people like us because there were not many houses available for rent due to the superstorm that demolished many homes a couple of years earlier. The load got very heavy for us and

I brought it to the Lord in prayer and asked Him to bring us another house to rent. I kept my trust in Him and believed that He would do it again–and He did (1 Timothy 4:10).

I was working at the medical office one day and a patient came in and asked, "Do you know anybody who wants to rent a house?" I literally screamed, "Yes, me." Her eyes got big and with a smile on her face, she said, "Really?" And we started to talk about business. I went home so excited about it as our lease was coming to an end in two months. It was God's perfect timing once again. We went to see the house and loved the inside. It had four bedrooms, but because we were used to living in a big two-story house, we were not sure about this one. This one was a ranch house. Honestly, I hated ranch houses. They were not my style, but it was what God wanted for me and my family, not what my preference was. I always ask God to change my desires that I would want what He wants for me, because He knows best. This house started to sit right in my heart. It was as if God was telling me to take this one. I started to talk my husband into it and we both decided to take it. When the time came, we signed the contract and moved in (Psalm 21:2).

I used to tell people that we downsized, until a friend of mine corrected me and said, "You right sized." That is when I realized that she was right. God opened a door that released us from the oppression of financial burden. It was the "right size and the right house" for my family, which we ended up buying years later.

Spending daily time with Jesus gives me something that I will never want to lose–that is discernment. One day, I could discern something about a specific lady, so I asked, "Is everything OK?" She told me she was battling cancer. How can I, a Christian, believer in Jesus Christ, knowing that the resurrection power of God is in me, do nothing for these people who are suffering with intense or terminal illness? Immediately, I introduced Jesus not just as a Savior, but as a healer and a miracle worker to this lady. With tears in her eyes, she received Him and her miracle–her healing. Months later, her husband came to me and said, "I want to thank you for what you did, you prayed for my wife and she came home completely different. Something happened that day and she is now cancer free." My answer to him of course was, "It's Jesus, he did it!" (Matthew 14:14).

An elderly man was battling a serious depression because of the loss of his wife. I prayed for him and kept encouraging him with the Word of God. He is now depression free and keeps telling me how I helped him through that hard time in his life. Of course, I keep pointing him and everybody else to the cross. To look up to Jesus because He is the one who does these miracles. I am just a vessel who makes myself available for Him to use (1 Peter 5:7).

An elderly Christian man asked me to pray for him. He was about to have open heart surgery. We put our faith together and asked our Father God for a miracle. This man came months later to share his amazing story. He said, "I died twice on the table and the surgeon brought me back." "What do you mean?" I asked. He explained, "When I was having the surgery, at one point, I felt this inexplicable peace. It was heaven. I know it was heaven. I wanted to stay there. I didn't see anything or hear anything, but I know my heart wanted to stay there, and then like in seconds, I was back to pain, grief, and disappointment. Then like ten minutes later, again, I was in that place of peace, complete peace. Again, I wanted to stay there so bad, but somehow, I was brought back to the pain and grieving. When I woke up from the surgery, the doctor told me that I died twice and that he brought me back. He explained to me that it happened about ten minutes apart. That is when I realized that was it. That was the moment when I felt that inexplicable peace. It was heaven. It was a beautiful feeling, but he brought me back." We were both laughing, amazed at his experience of Heaven. God is awesome (Psalm 19:1)!

This same man's wife was battling fear, panic, and anxiety. She confessed to me (with tears in her eyes) that she needed to have a very serious surgery, but she kept rescheduling the appointment because of fear. I told her about the love of God and introduced Jesus to her as a Savior and Prince of peace. She accepted Him as her Lord and Savior and instantly her face was glowing and, with a big smile on her face, she said, "I felt something lifted."

A certain lady who was battling terminal cancer came in one day, and for some reason, not even knowing her situation, my heart was full of compassion for her. I knew deep in my heart that she needed Jesus. I asked her, "Can I pray for you?" Immediately, she said, "Yes." That day something unexplainable happened. I prayed a prayer that transformed her heart. The Spirit of God was in that room. She cried so much that at the end she thanked me for the peace that came upon her heart. She kept saying how much she needed it. She came back many other times with her husband who was a very serious man; he never talked and sometimes came across as a very angry man. However, she always had something funny to say and made me laugh. There was one specific time, as she was leaving, I felt in my heart that it was time for her to say the prayer of receiving Jesus as her Lord and Savior. While I was deciding if I should go talk to her about it or not, she continued walking. She was outside and I saw the top of her head while passing through a window. Finally, she was in the parking lot. At that point, I thought it was too late, and decided not to tell her about Christ. I watched her drive away. Honestly, I felt bad. I wanted her to repeat the salvation prayer but it did not happen. I was too busy or too lazy to get up and talk to her. It was heavy on my heart for a moment, but knowing God, I knew that He does not condemn me because of this, so I let it go and moved on (Romans 8:1; Psalm 32:5).

Weeks later, I called to confirm her appointment and her husband answered the phone. I could tell by the tone of his voice that he was crying. I asked, "Is everything OK?" He responded, "Oh honey, my wife passed away and today is her funeral. You called on a very sad day." "Oh no. I'm sorry!" I said. He began to cry so loud. He was devastated. Automatically, I started to remind him of all the funny things she did when she came to visit and told him that this is the way we will always remember her, and he started to laugh. I felt a change in the atmosphere, he was now telling me funny things that she did at home. Laughter is medicine to our bones. I had no other words to encourage him except the Word of God. Our conversation came to a point where I introduced Jesus to him, and he received Him as his Lord and Savior. Next, I asked something that blew my mind, "Do you have a Bible?" His response, "You know, it's funny that you ask because right before you called, I was looking at different things in our room and in a drawer I found a Bible, and I thought that I should read it." "There you go, I'm just confirming that. Yes, you should read it," I responded, and he agreed as we said goodbye (Proverbs 16:9).

This man surprised me one day; he came in and was the happiest man on the planet. He was laughing and making jokes. We were astonished by this. What happened? We all questioned one another. The Word of God changes everything. It is powerful like a double-edged sword and it penetrates the heart (Hebrews 4:12).

What exactly happened here? Sometimes I would think that this woman did receive Jesus as her Savior the day that I prayed for her because she really was broken and cried deeply. Something different happened that day; she even confirmed that. But because she didn't repeat the prayer of salvation, in my mind, she was not saved. When I heard that she passed away, oh my, I felt horrible. But then her husband not only said the prayer, but he started to read the Word and it was manifesting in him. My only explanation of all of this is that sometimes we put our hope and security in a confession of words for salvation, when salvation is more than just that. It is something deep. It is repentance from the heart. It is a turnaround from our sins. It is the brokenness of our heart recognizing that we are sinners and that we need Jesus as our Lord and Savior. I myself repeated the prayer outwardly from my lips earlier in life, but not from my heart. After that prayer, I continued living my life in sin, nothing changed, until that genuine and raw moment of conviction. A moment of an authentic encounter with Christ. That moment when I admitted that I was wrong. I was not a victim, but I was a sinner and that I needed a Savior and I asked God for His forgiveness (Ephesians 2:8–9; Titus 3:5; Romans 10:9).

That same week, a friend of mine shared her experience with me, without knowing anything about my own experience. She said, "My friend was very sick, fighting terminal cancer and I went to visit her at the hospital. I knew that I needed to share about salvation with her. She wasn't saved and I didn't. I went home feeling very guilty about that and the next morning, I found out that she passed away. I felt worse, guilt and condemnation tormented me very badly because of her soul. I went to her funeral, and when I was looking at her dead body, deep in my heart I was asking God to forgive me for not bringing her to Christ and I promised to Him that from that moment on I would talk about Jesus to every person in my path. Immediately, at that very moment, a totally strange woman came and kneeled next to me. I started to feel that I needed to keep the promise I had made just seconds before, and I, with boldness, looked at the woman next to me and asked, 'Are you saved?' And she responded, 'Yes, I'm a Christian,' and began to explain to me how she introduced Jesus to my friend the night before she died. I jumped with joy. My guilt and condemnation disappeared right away." (John 3:17).

This explained everything for me, Salvation is by grace (Ephesians 1:7). God will not put the responsibility of salvation of each soul on us. He is perfect in all of His ways. He will have ways and can speak to different hearts about ministering to each person on this planet. Of course, it is extremely important for us to share the gospel and carry out the commission we are commanded, but salvation does not depend on us, or near-memorized and simplified repeating of words. "No one can come to me unless the Father who sent me draws them, and I will raise them up on the last day" (John 6:44).

Another experience I must share is about a lady who was always mean and angry. It was like when you see or smell a skunk, you want to run away and hide, that is how bad she was. But I could not run away or hide. As a Christian, I decided to love on her because love, perfect love, God's love, covers a multitude of sins and casts out fear. I paid good for evil, and when she "forced me to go one mile, I went two" (1 John 4:18; 1 Peter 4:8).

One specific time, she yelled and insulted me terribly over the phone. A day later, she came to the office and I knew that, as always, she needed my physical help to get out of her car. I decided that day was the day of salvation for her. I went and first greeted her with a big smile on my face, and a happy, joyful, and willing heart, as I helped her. She could not even look me in my eyes. I realized that she was crying, and I asked, "Is anything wrong?" and she responded, "Yes, I have been wrong. I'm sorry. I don't know why I always treat people like that." I began to minister to her heart by saying that people only give what they have in their heart, that hurting people hurt people. She looked at me and asked, "Are you a minister?" "No, I'm not, but my husband is," I said. She cried even more, saying, "Oh God, I have been so terrible to a minister's wife." I explained to her that I was just a person like her and our conversation led to salvation. She received Jesus as her Lord and Savior. Amazingly, she asked me what church I attend, and when I told her, she was astonished and explained to me, "That church has been feeding me and my mom for years. My mom goes to pick up food from their food pantry every month." God is amazing! But see, this makes me think, what if I allowed the words of this woman to penetrate my heart and repay her wrong for wrong? I would not be used for her freedom. For me, deep in my heart, this is a major joy, to see people coming to the light of Jesus Christ and seeing them being freed from the bondage of Satan. I can relate with people because I was once in darkness, a blind guide leading the blinded, but now I can see and I can help others to come to the light. To enter the small gate and narrow road that leads to life and that only few find it (Luke 6:39; John 9:25; Matthew 7:14).

During a very cold winter one morning, the Lord opened a door for me to talk to my boss at work about giving. I told him that according to my experiences, it feels better when we give than when we receive. I shared a story of a church that ordered food at a pizza place, and unexpectedly they blessed the delivery man with so much money that he was crying and was so thankful to God for it. Minutes later, someone came into the waiting room. It was a man who clearly looked homeless. He asked if he could sit in the waiting room for a little bit and I said, "Yes." My boss looked at him and, full of compassion, he asked me to warm a can of soup he had in his office to give it to the man in the waiting room. I slowly walked towards the man with the hot soup in my hands and I said, "Sir, this is for you." At that moment something happened. I first looked at his dirty shoes and could discern something that I cannot explain. It was as if something spiritual was about to happen. I gave him the soup and asked, "Would you mind if we pray?" He said, "Yes," and I not only thanked God for the food, but I prayed for this man also. After all of this, he looked at me and said, "May the Lord bless you." Those words stayed with me forever. "May the Lord bless you" (Colossians 1:26–27).

We continued going about our normal day as he was still seated in the waiting room. My greatest concern was our next patient; she was a very sophisticated lady. I did not know what her reaction would be when she saw and smelled this man sitting there. What would she and other patients think, I wondered? But to my surprise, she came in, and while standing at the check-in window, she could not talk. She was sobbing. "What happened?" I asked. She whispered, "Is that man a homeless person?" "I think so," I responded. She cried more. She came in and out crying and said that she did not know why she was feeling that way. This lady and her husband accepted Jesus as their Lord and Savior years before (Jeremiah 33:3).

This was a different type of day. I could feel something in the atmosphere. We had many chairs all around the waiting room. That man chose to sit in the chair that was back across the window from the front desk, where I could stare straight at him. Many people came in and out that day and the man sat in the waiting room the whole day. I kept looking to see if he was still there. Our normal and natural concern was that he would get so comfortable that he would come back every day. He said nothing, but just sat there very quietly for many hours (1 Corinthians 4:1).

Our last patient left and we were finally done for the day, I looked to see if he was still there and he was. I began to feel bad because we would have to tell him to leave. At that moment my boss asked me, "Is that man still there?" I looked one more time to make sure and said, "Yes." He walked towards the waiting room with the intention to tell him that he had to leave. I quickly looked through the front desk window one more time but he was gone! Gone! Oh my, what happened? He was gone! Where did he go? How did he leave? We both were astonished. The building has an alarm that tells us when someone walks in or out of the building, but no alarm sounded. We walked outside looking to see if he was walking in front or in the back of the building but he was not. It was as if he just disappeared. We both testified about witnessing this amazing thing. There is no explanation for any of this (Colossians 1:16).

I went home and shared this experience with my family, and just minutes later, I received a phone call. It was my boss's wife asking, "What exactly happened today at the office? My husband came home crying. Tell me what happened." I told her the whole story and she said, "Glennys, you had a visitation, that was an angel and is in the Bible." (Hebrews 13:2).

I could not believe it. That has stuck in my heart forever. We never saw this man again. He never returned to the dental office, but we kept it all in our hearts. I personally agree with my friend who said that that was a visitation of the Lord (Genesis 18:1–5).

Being in a relationship with God has transformed my heart. I have always given Him the first priority in my life because He alone is worthy. I am His sheep and I recognize His voice. I learned to walk by the Spirit. I allow Him to use me the way He wants to. I am aware that I cannot create a miracle. It is God who does it. I am just His willing vessel. I learned to walk in love, hope, kindness, compassion, and overall, wisdom. I learned to surrender and to die daily to my own self, my own thinking, and my own desires, to faithfully please God before man. Always asking for not my will, but God's will be done here on earth as it is in heaven. I want to be different, to be set-apart, to be holy as He is holy (John 10:1–5; 1 Peter 1:16)!

I believe God and I expect Him to move through me each day. My expectations are not only on Sunday, but every day of the week. "This is the day the Lord has made and I will rejoice and be glad in it" (Psalm 118:24).

I love God's presence. I love to worship Him; I love to read His Word and allow Him to speak to my heart. He speaks truth at all times because He is truth, regardless of how I feel, or how I take it. He always shows me "Me," my own heart and His intentions for me are always the best, but it is up to me if I take it or leave it. He never stops changing me, correcting me, or transforming my heart. He never gives up on me because He loves me. This is how I know that I am far from perfect and that I need Him every day in my life. I honestly do not want to be "Me," I want to represent Him at all times. I want Him to teach me how to be a wife, a mother, a sister, a friend, and overall, a Christian. It is in that secret place that I find my strength, my refuge, my identity, who I am and who He is–He is the "I AM" and He is "REAL" (John 14:6; 2 Timothy 3:16; Hebrews 12:5–11; Exodus 3:14).

He wants us to heal the sick and set captives free. What is so amazing to me is that in my place of work, I always had to work hard as I took on more responsibilities. I cover many different positions; however, I started to hold back a little bit in praying for people because they were getting healed and restored so often,

I thought that it could get me in trouble. I guess this is a good problem to have (Isaiah 61:1; Isaiah 41:10).

One day, a lady came in crying in terrible pain. I could not help it. It bothers me to see people suffering. I hate sickness. It is an oppression from Hell (Matthew 4:24). The compassion in my heart became greater after I was the one suffering sickness in my own body years before. I asked this lady if I could pray for her and she said, "Yes." I prayed in the name of Jesus and instantly she was healed. But now there was another problem. She came to see the doctor because of the pain and it was gone. "What do I do now?" she asked. I told her to see the doctor to confirm that it was gone. Honestly, I felt funny about this. I truly do not want my boss to think that I am taking his job away by using the healing power of God. This lady saw him and had an X-ray done. I was blown away to hear the report. He said, "I don't see anything, if it continues, come back to see us." She came out and she likewise was astonished and looked at me with a big smile on her face and said, "I am amazed; what just happened?" "It is simple. You were healed by the power of Jesus Christ," I responded (Isaiah 53:4–5; Jeremiah 30:17).

Another precious lady came in a different time and it was obvious that she was fighting a sickness. She could not walk or talk right. She was fighting Parkinson's disease. "Can I pray for you?" I asked. "Yes, please," she responded. At that moment, she received Jesus as her Lord and Savior. I prayed for her and she went home. A month later, the same lady came back and I greeted her as normal, "Good morning. How are you?" With a big smile, she responded, "Healed! Do you remember me?" "Yes," I responded. She continued, "That day you prayed for me, something happened. The next day I woke up completely healed. I know it was a miracle as you said. I visited my doctor and he said that the medicine was supposed to help my symptoms, not to heal me. I told the doctor it wasn't the medicine. It was Jesus that gave me a miracle." We rejoiced together. I was just overwhelmed by God's amazing love for people (Proverbs 4:20–22).

One time a patient did not show up to his appointment. When the doctor realized that he did not see him yet, he asked me if I prayed for this patient? At first, I did not understand what he was asking, until he laughed and asked again, "Did you pray for him?" What he meant was if the patient went home healed because of my prayer. At this point, it was obvious that God was doing something in this place (Ephesians 3:20).

A man for some reason could not swallow. He was getting very anxious and so we called 911. The man grabbed his neck and kept repeating, "I can't swallow! I can't swallow!" I couldn't help it, I asked him, "Sir. can I pray for you in the name of Jesus?" He said "Yes, please!" After I prayed, I grabbed a cup of water and handed it to him, and he swallowed fine. He could not stop saying, "It's gone. I'm fine, I'm fine!" The doctor walked into the room and immediately I left the room feeling as If I just broke a rule or did something wrong in the eyes of men, but not in God's eyes. I overheard the man saying to the doctor, "She prayed for me and I'm fine now." While silently rejoicing, I opened the door for the EMT that arrived. I sat quietly at the front desk behind the computer, observing the whole scene of officers and EMT personnel walking in with all of their equipment to help a man that Jesus already healed. Minutes later, I saw them one by one leave. The doctor called me in to help perform the work this man came in for. The patient left like nothing ever happened (Mark 9:23; John 14:12). I have to admit that I was nervous about what my boss would say, but to my surprise his response, after I apologized for praying for the man was, "Prayer works, prayer works!"

God has been faithful to watch over His Word to perform it in me and through me. I am just a person who believes God. There are times that we need a certain amount of money for specific needs. In response to prayer, we still receive calls from faithful people who we met over the years, who are unaware of our needs, saying that they want to plant significant financial seeds in our life. God has my family and all of our needs covered. I do not have to worry about tomorrow, what we will eat, or what we will wear because more than working for a man, I am working for the kingdom of God. He is the one who takes care of me and my family (Jeremiah 1:12; Matthew 6:34).

During this time, as all of these things were happening, our ministry had been successfully growing. Shawn had become the face of *Move the Earth*, reversing the trend of biblical unbelief by teaching and preaching biblical unity and worldview clarity. God began to show us that there was one significant element that was missing here in the beautiful State of New Jersey and among our brothers and sisters in Christ. This was missing among churches, among the body of Christ, and that is unity–a house divided, cannot stand (Mark 3:25).

God began to use the ministry to bring that great element back to its place–the church. There was so much division, anger, jealousy, unforgiveness. It was as if an enemy came in and planted a bad seed–weeds among the wheat (Matthew 13:25).

These pastors and leaders started getting together every month to fellowship and to pray together as one, and unity naturally started to take place. They started to know each other more and more, and to see each other not as competitors, but as brothers and sisters of the same body, same army, same team, regardless of their differences, or their way of worship (1 Corinthians 1:10; Ephesians 4:1–6).

Shawn, by the wisdom of God, brought to their focus the things that united them and not the things that separated them. We began to do what Jesus did with the woman at the well. She was focusing on their differences, on the things that separated them. "You are a Jew and I'm a Samaritan," she said. But Jesus said to her, "Woman, believe me, a time is coming when you will worship the Father neither on this mountain nor in Jerusalem. You Samaritans worship what you do not know; we worship what we do know, for salvation is from the Jews. Yet a time is coming and has now come when the true worshipers will worship the Father in the Spirit and in truth, for they are the kind of worshipers the Father seeks. God is spirit, and his worshippers must worship in the Spirit and in truth" (John 4:21–24).

We started to focus on the five core beliefs that bring us together in unity as one body:

1–God is the Creator and is sovereign over His creation.

2–The Bible is 100% true and its moral teachings apply today.

3–The devil is real and not merely a symbol of evil.

4–Man is sinful and saved by grace.

5–Jesus is the sinless Savior, the Son of God.

God is a promise keeper. Remember the promise He gave me when I told Him that I wanted to meet my two nephews, the children of my brother who tragically passed away years before in Texas? Well, somehow God opened a door for Shawn to support the nation of Israel by becoming the New Jersey State Director of a pro-Israel organization. Who would think this would happen this way? Only the one and true God! I will bless those who bless you, and whoever curses you I will curse (Genesis 12:3). The founder of this organization resides in the great state of Texas. In the beginning of this specific year, fourteen years after my brother passed, Shawn and I were invited to attend one of their events in Texas. We were both very excited about this. A week before our trip, I was praying when God brought to my remembrance the promise He gave me when He said, "One day I will bring you to meet them." And that time was now. The only means of contact I found was the social media account of my nephews' grandmother. I asked her to please help me to make this possible and she did. That same day, their mother contacted me and agreed to come to the hotel that we were going to stay at to visit with my two nephews. I could not believe it. I called my whole family and told them what was about to happen. I knew that this was a promise that was about to come to pass. In prayer, I felt that God wanted me to bring them some gifts and among those gifts, a Bible (Isaiah 40:8).

That day before our trip, I texted my nephew's mother, letting her know that we were leaving the next morning. I was concerned because I did not hear back from her. It made me feel nervous, but I kept my faith. We got there and I texted her again, and still I had no response. At that point, I shared with Shawn and he tried to encourage me by saying, "She might not come, but it is OK, there will be another opportunity." Immediately, I shut him down and said, "Nope, I don't think so. This is a promise and regardless of how it looks, I believe God" (Acts 27:25).

The next day, I took another step and I called her, still no response. I started to get a little bit anxious about it. It is here when my spirit began a war against my natural mind. "Shut up, devil, and get behind me. This is a promise and God will bring it to pass." I kept my faith and believed God, regardless of the situation. Later on that day, before the service started, I met a wonderful lady, who has become my friend since that moment. I shared with her about the whole situation. She added her faith to mine and we prayed, commanding the devil and anything else to move out of the way and we started to praise God and give Him the glory for it in Jesus' name. The service started minutes later. I had my phone on vibration mode expecting her to call me and I did not want to miss it (Matthew 18:19).

The founder's son was giving the Word at that moment and he said things like, "God is not a man that he should lie. He didn't bring you here for nothing. He will do what he promised because he is a promise keeper. You and your family shall be saved!" I did not need any more confirmation. I was not imagining things; it was God who brought me here and it was for a reason. This was very important for me and for my family. It was at that moment that my phone vibrated. I grabbed it and ran out. Yes, it was her!

She acknowledged that she was struggling with this reunion but decided to come to visit that next day (Matthew 21:22).

That morning, I could not stop thanking God for what was about to happen. His promise was about to come to pass. A closure many years in the making was about to take place. My heart was pounding. The waiting and anxious moments were about to come to an end. I was at the door of the hotel, when I saw her coming out of her car with my two nephews all grown, and her boyfriend. We hugged and cried as if we had so much to express, but our emotions could not control themselves. Then, the moment came, one by one I met and hugged my nephews. This was the promise God gave me and it came to pass. They all came inside the room at the hotel, and God, as always, went above and beyond what we could imagine (Ephesians 3:20).

We started to talk about different things and I gave them their gifts, including the Bibles. Our conversation got deeper and deeper and brought us to talk about that day my brother and she came to visit my family in Ohio just for one night. "What happened that day?" she asked. I responded, "Remember when I asked my brother if he knew Jesus as his Lord and Savior and he responded, Yes! I received him years ago with my father and now I want to find a church and serve him"? "Yes, I remember," she said. I addressed to all of them how important accepting Jesus as our Lord and Savior is. It is because of Christ that my brother made it to Heaven. They were all listening very carefully. I continued to explain about salvation by using my brother as an example. He did not know that he was going to die that young. No one knows when it is our time and that is why it is extremely important for us to make this decision while we are alive. The people who do not make it to Heaven are those who rejected Jesus as their Lord and Savior. "Where would you like to spend eternity?" I asked. I continued saying, "It is up to us. I'm extremely happy that my brother made the right decision while he was alive because dead people can't decide because it is too late, they're dead." And it was at that moment that I asked them if they would like to do the same as my brother did–give their lives to God and receive His Son Jesus as their Lord and Savior? It was quiet, you could hear a pin drop for a second, and then, one by one they said, "I do!" (Romans 10:9; Joshua 24:15).

All of them, including her boyfriend, received Jesus as their Lord and Savior right in the hotel room. God gave me a word of knowledge for her boyfriend. He was sobbing, asking her how I knew things about his life. She kept saying, "She doesn't know, I didn't see her for years, it's God." (Daniel 2:22) That day God also ministered to the heart of my older nephew to bring clarity and reconciliation between him and his mother. They cried, hugged and kissed each other (Ephesians 4:32).

Then, three more amazing moments happened. God is so powerful. I explained to them that what they just did, receiving Jesus as their Lord and Savior is the key to enter Heaven. I asked the question that changed everything, "Do you know that this means that when you die you are going to Heaven and who will you see there?" "God," they responded. "Yes,', I said, "But who else?" They all looked at me waiting for me to tell them. I could not stop crying because this right here is a promise that comes with the salvation of Jesus Christ. This is the comfort that brings peace to our broken hearts. This right here brought joy to these young men. "You will see your father, my brother, in heaven one day. We will all be back together one day!" Oh their faces, their smiles, it was as hope and peace just came into their hearts. For this I am forever thankful to God, to this organization, and to my husband Shawn for his obedience to allow God to guide his steps (1 Thessalonians 4:13–18).

Next, I looked at my youngest nephew and asked, "Do you know why your father wanted you to have the name that you have?" "No, why?" he asked. I responded with tears in my eyes, the same words as my brother. Words that I carried for fourteen years deep in my heart to be released at a moment I didn't even know, but that moment was now, "He wanted you to be called that name because it is in the Bible and he wanted you to have a biblical name." He immediately grabbed the Bible I just gave him and began to flip the pages so fast because he could not wait to see his name written in that book. While flipping through the pages, he asked, "Where? Where?" I grabbed the Bible from him and I opened it right to the book in the New Testament that bears his name, and I gave it back to him. He grabbed it with so much passion and repeated his name aloud while reading it. I can tell you that this moment brought his heart closure not just to his natural father, but to God. What a point of connection. God's plans are completely amazing (Jeremiah 1:5)!

I then turned my attention to their mother and broke into tears, another special moment came. A moment where it was time to reveal a secret I carried for fourteen years. This was not planned; everything just happened. It was at this moment that I realized, by the Spirit of God, that this was a specific moment of truth. What a closure God did here this day. I asked my nephews' mother, "Remember that day while you were swimming at the pool that my brother whispered something in my ear, and you asked me, what did he say? I never told you what he secretly whispered to me, but now is the time. I want you to know his secret. She fell apart right there. She cried so much because she remembered very clearly that moment and knowing what he said would bring so many answers and closure to her heart (Psalm 147:3).

I proceeded to say, "What he told me was, "I love her so much. She is the love of my life and she doesn't even know it." This was so significant for her and her children's lives. We all had such a good time together and more than a closure for them, it was a much-needed closure for me in many different ways. Now there was finally peace like a river. I have delivered every word and every message I carried for my brother and from God to bring his family to the kingdom of God through the salvation of Jesus Christ. God, you did it. Even when I did not see it, you were working (Philippians 4:6–7)!

Shawn was still doing the ministry of *Move the Earth*, at the same time he was working for the pro-Israel organization, and people continued supporting our call more and more. Around this time, a great burden began on Shawn's heart, and that is the protection of Christian values and prayer and intercession for New Jersey. I supported my husband 100% and prayed even harder because we both have always had the same concerns in our hearts. We fight the good fight of faith together, regardless of our differences. The main thing in all of this is that even though we are naturally two different individuals, because of our individual daily relationship with God our Father, we became one in spirit. We always, let me repeat that, we always hear God's voice the same, and we are so grateful for that. God is our rock, the foundation of our life and our marriage. We do our best to follow His decrees and are careful to obey His commands (John 15:5; Leviticus 26:2–8).

This time has been a training field for me. I learned so much. God has always used my husband, Shawn, to teach me submission to God and overall humility. I allow God to do the work in my heart and in the heart of others. The most important ingredient for unity is in Philippians 2:3. Instead of being motivated by selfish ambition or vanity, each of you should, in humility, be moved to treat one another as more important than yourself.

It was here where I started to ask for more. I felt as if what I was doing was not enough. "God, I want to *Move the Earth* more. Why do you give me this life, this relationship with you, all of these experiences and for what? To keep it inside. God, I want more!"

One thing that started to grow at this time was a desire in my heart to share with the entire world the amazing experiences I had, so the world would know that God is real. I kept praying and I have to admit that sometimes I complained to Shawn saying, "God is doing nothing with me. Why does he fill me up, for what? To keep it inside. I feel like I'm going to explode. I want to be used at a different level ... Yata-yata-yata ... "

My heart was itching and to be honest, I could go and do my own thing, that we all know very well how to do, and it may work, but is that what God wants me to do? I know the difference in right from wrong and good from evil. I learned to submit to the voice of God and to obey Him, regardless of my feelings, ideas and desires. His son purchased me with His blood. I once was a slave of Satan and I sinned very well, but now I am a slave of Jesus Christ and I want to do my job for Him very well also, so I always wait to hear His instruction for me to follow. He is my helper and all my best ideas are His. I kept diligently seeking Him (Proverbs 8:17). I seek His presence continually (1 Chronicles 16:11)!

Finally, what Shawn told me two or three years before when he heard God telling him what was going to happen, came to pass. He was asked to take the position as the Director of a Pro-Family Advocacy Organization–standing for our Christian values (Lamentations 3:37; Daniel 4:17)!

Prayerfully, Shawn took the responsibility that God put on his heart and let go of everything else, including *Move the Earth*. We both thought that it was time to lay our baby down, as Abraham did Isaac. At one point, we even thought that He provided the ram (someone to take over this ministry). We were bringing a friend from South Carolina to do the work. Everything was in pointing that direction and we were very happy about it, but suddenly things started to change (Genesis 22:1–18).

It was here that I started to feel that I was the one supposed to take this responsibility. I heard God ask, "Are you done with the book yet?" His plan is amazing. Every detail just makes me speechless. Years ago, God put the desire on my heart to write down every experience I had with Him. He even confirmed this with my good friends from Ohio who told me that I was going to write a book. I did start with this assignment, but then I stopped and did not continue. I even asked this friend of mine if she could do it for me, that I was going to tell her about every experience and she would write it. That is how we do things sometimes. We want God to call us. Call me, God, call me. And then we want to give someone else the responsibilities that comes with the call. Sometimes I wonder if we are really serious about asking God to call us into ministry or to walk on water as Peter did. And where are our expectations? Are we really waiting, ready, expecting that moment when God says, "It is your time to shine. It is your time to run the race." For me, I was not ready. I went crazy and frustrated. How many times God tells us to start doing something and because in our own eyes it does not make sense, or it is not that easy, or is not working the way we think it should work, we leave it, forget it, and quit? But not God, He always finishes what He starts (1 Corinthians 9:24–27)!

Now He was asking me, "Where is it? Where is the book?" My answer was, "Oh, God, I am sorry. I thought that was not going to work, so I put it on the side." My to-do list increased at this time. God asked me to finish the book and that it was time for me to come out of the shell. Time to stop hiding behind my husband and to take leadership of the ministry. That same week in a meeting, the board of directors of *Move the Earth* requested the same–for me to continue the torch of the ministry. Fear started to come into my heart. No, I can't. I was saying to myself. Even the pastors from the Undivided Prayer meeting asked for me to become the face of *Move the Earth*. That was nice of them, but I just did not know how I could do what Shawn does. It was impossible for me to do that (Proverbs 3:4; Luke 18:27).

This time in my life I cried like never before. This cry would come out of nowhere and for nothing. I just could not stop crying. I could not understand what was happening. Why was I feeling as if something was happening inside of me? I have to admit that I almost ran like Jonah, hiding from my call. I honestly preferred to be inside the belly of a big fish, than doing what God wanted me to do. Even though my heart has always been for ministry, I just could not find myself fitting in this position because in my mind I was seeing it as if I was going to be Shawn, to do exactly what he did and that was impossible for me in many ways. My struggle was saying "no" to God because I did not trust my abilities and capacity to do what He was calling me to do (Psalm 56:8–9).

I finally asked God to help my weakness. I recognized in His presence that I was afraid and that I did not know how to do this. Right there, God said to me, "*Move the Earth* is transitioning into a prayer and intercession ministry." And that was it. I was plugged in at that moment, because that is me. That is who I am–a prayer and intercessory warrior. Now we are talking, Lord. Now we meant business (Psalm 44:21)!

That same day, Shawn said to me, "*Move the Earth* is transitioning into a prayer and intercession ministry." Wow … What a confirmation for me. Then I called a friend and I told her the whole thing and how afraid I was before. She said something that encouraged me even more, "Glennys, you won't do what Shawn does. You will be YOU and you are bringing a different element to the ministry." (Psalm 139:14–16).

And as if that wasn't enough, I called another friend, the same woman who years before came to my house speaking in tongues and who washed my feet. I asked her to pray for me. I did not tell her anything that was happening when she started to pray. She paused and said, "*Move the Earth* is transitioning into a prayer and intercession ministry." That was it for me. Now I knew that this was my call because I am in my field. Thanks to our pastor's mother at the church in Ohio (chapter 4), who imparted to me this amazing gift–the fire of prayer, this is what I know how to do the most. As David was trained to kill giants by killing the bear and the lion, I, too, have been equipped all these years and trained with the armor of prayer and intercession that has killed many giants in my path. When God called David to kill Goliath, Saul gave him his armor to wear, but it did not fit David because Saul's armor was too big and too heavy for David to wear. He knew that he could not defeat the enemy wearing Saul's armor, so he took it off and refused to wear it. He was trained in a different way than Saul's army and therefore he wore a different armor to defeat his enemies. He had what he needed—five smooth stones and his sling, and with that David killed Goliath. It was the same with me; Shawn's armor could not fit me, it was too big and too heavy. I have been equipped and trained these years with a different armor, the one that fits me perfectly and is all I need to defeat the enemy (1 Samuel 17)!

I am a soldier in the army of the Most High God, my commander in chief, and I am in this world equipped with armor to fight the good fight of faith until He calls me home and tells me "Well done, good and faithful servant."

I AM REAL!

Review–I had two different turns in my life–The plan of Satan (death) and the plan of God (life). I chose life by dying to my own desires and my own thinking. I live by faith and see things through the eyes of God, not my natural eyes. I'm not my own, but His. I want to see His will done here on earth as it is in heaven, and for many to believe and not perish. The purpose of life is to share about the salvation that is found in Jesus Christ alone.

Encouragement–Never give up. Don't quit. If you have to hang on one nail, you hang on one nail because you are not alone. You are made with courage and for a purpose. You were perfectly created in your mother's womb regardless of your circumstances.

Apply–John 16:33; Philippians 4:13; Mark 5:36; 1 Corinthians 10:13; Psalm 16:8; John 14:27; Romans 15:13; Exodus 15:2; 1 Chronicles 16:11; 2 Timothy 1:7; 2 Corinthians 12:9–10; Isaiah 40:29.

Learned–I learned to have nothing and to have everything in both stages of life. I am still a winner because the joy, happiness, and riches of Christ in me–the hope of glory!